LEONIDAS MERRITT

SEVEN IRON MEN

The Fesler–Lampert Minnesota Heritage Book Series

This series reprints significant books that enhance our understanding and appreciation of Minnesota and the Upper Midwest. It is supported by the generous assistance of the John K. and Elsie Lampert Fesler Fund and the interest and contribution of Elizabeth P. Fesler and the late David R. Fesler.

SEVEN IRON MEN

The Merritts and the Discovery of the Mesabi Range

PAUL DE KRUIF

University of Minnesota Press
Minneapolis
London

Originally published as *Seven Iron Men* by Harcourt, Brace and Company. Copyright 1929 by Harcourt, Brace and Company, Inc.; copyright renewed 1957 by Paul de Kruif.

First University of Minnesota Press edition, 2007

Published by the University of Minnesota Press
111 Third Avenue South, Suite 290
Minneapolis, MN 55401-2520
http://www.upress.umn.edu

LIBRARY OF CONGRESS CATALOGING-IN-PUBLICATION DATA
De Kruif, Paul, 1890-1971.
Seven iron men : the Merritts and the discovery of the Mesabi Range /
Paul de Kruif.
p. cm. — (The Fesler–Lampert Minnesota heritage book series)
Includes bibliographical references and index.
ISBN-13: 978-0-8166-5262-4 (pb : alk. paper)
ISBN-10: 0-8166-5262-7 (pb : alk. paper)
1. Merritt family. 2.Merritt, Leonidas, 1844–1926. 3. Iron mines and
mining—Minnesota. 4. Mesabi Range (Minn.) I. Title.
TN403.M6D4 2007
6221.3410977677—dc22
[B] 2007028814

Printed in the United States of America on acid-free paper

The University of Minnesota is an equal-opportunity educator
and employer.

15 14 13 12 11 10 09 08 07   10 9 8 7 6 5 4 3 2 1

AGAIN
TO RHEA

MOTTO

"There is a romance about iron . . . I wonder if the courageous men who seek it in the bowels of the earth realize their big part in the life of the world? Do the brave, bare bodies, that reflect the furnace light and the gloating glow of the smelter, do their work because of a subtle subconsciousness of the fact that the wheels of the world and civilization would stop if they stopped?

"Iron ore and steel are of greater importance than wheat, because there are many good substitutes for wheat. There is none for iron ore. It has a glory of usefulness all its own. Those who are associated with its production should know of the dignity of their calling; should realize it and then their hearts and souls would fill their big bodies until brawn and spirit are one, as an instrument of the joy of existence in the keen sense of service. There would be a brotherhood of iron that could not know strife if the totality of performance could be shown to the eyes of all those who inhabit the world of steel. . . ."

CHASE SALMON OSBORN

ACKNOWLEDGMENTS

To W. E. Culkin and the staff of the St. Louis County Historical Society, my thanks for their generosity and kindness in directing me to obscure sources of information dealing with the pioneer history of the Head of the Lakes, and for placing at my disposal their conveniently arranged data that reveal the story of the pioneer days of this important region.

To Chase S. Osborn, my gratitude: first for his preceptorship in the early days of my studies, in "Little Duck" on *Zheshebe Minis,* leading to the writing of this tale; then for his generosity in making clear to me the spirit of those iron hunters, a nearly dead race now, of which the mighty Osborn himself is one of the last; and finally for his magnificent conception of Lake Superior sitting "in a rim of iron."

To Philip S. Rose, especially my thanks: for certain stories told me between midnight and dawn, revealing an America fashioned in remote aeons by the Inscrutable Forces of Nature, for reasons unknown, long before there were men to inhabit or use it. To this philosopher, too, my gratitude

ix

ACKNOWLEDGMENTS

for his tolerance of my especial pre-occupation with the hopes, struggles, strangely forgotten achievements of these seven iron men—whose lives, Rose forces me to admit, are in the long run unimportant, are hardly so much as a heartbeat in the life of the American Continent.

Bronxville,
April 14, 1929

CONTENTS

ILLUSTRATIONS

ILLUSTRATIONS

PART ONE

ANDANTE

"At each succeeding spring we whistled with the blackbirds and sang with the robins because we knew—"

LEONIDAS MERRITT

I

THOUGH Hepzibeth Merritt weighed hardly more than a hundred pounds, she was remarkable for being the mother of eight boys, all husky, and of one boy and a girl who died: she was the mother and grandmother of the seven iron men whose rise and fall this story tells. In the year 1856 this wiry dame—after the manner of her breed and the fashion of her times—set sail from mild, corn-fed Ohio towards the steel-gray water of Lake Superior, of Kitchi Gammi, of the great cold Lake that sits so strangely in a rim of iron.

By a coincidence this straight-lipped slip of a frontier woman set her face toward the north, toward vast, mysteriously hidden stores of cheap iron ore, in the very year that the Englishman, Henry Bessemer, started to transform the world by his famous simple trick of turning iron into cheap tough steel. By a succession of events most fortunate for our American land, Hepzibeth Merritt set out for the foggy north where this red and blue and purple ore lay hidden, some thirty-five years before the furnaces of Andrew Carnegie needed it, before the forges of the new-born United States Steel Corporation demanded it, before America absolutely required it to smelt for plows and sewing machines, for motors, steel rails and suspension bridges, for her skyscrapers that now rise like a hundred thousand towers of Babel, in short—for her whole arrogant age of steel—

Of all this Hepzibeth was ignorant; she only took her five youngest boys—to say nothing of the ancient black Merritt cow—and sailed northward up that chain of wide blue ponds of water left by an ice cap that melted at an ancient time of nobody knows how many thousands of years ago. With never a thought of iron at all, save that her man must have it for his saws, her boys for their plows and axes, the stern and gentle Hepzibeth sailed up these blue twisting liquid lanes of dirt-cheap traffic on a forgotten side-wheel steamboat whose mate rejoiced in the name of Big-mouth Charley. She may not have wanted to go north; she had to, willy-nilly, to tidy the log-house and fry the whitefish for her husband, Lewis Howell Merritt—a man of extremes—who had taken up a squatter's claim at the Head of the Lakes the year before.

I say this iron-shouldered father of the iron men was a man of extremes, because of his utterly unexplainable conduct in leaving Chautauqua County in York State, then Warren County in western

Pennsylvania, then rich-soiled Ohio, to come to Duluth—a rocky, God-forgotten corner of the northwest world—to ply his trade of millwright and sawmill man. Northeastward from the tip of this fog-shrouded water that lies in a mysterious gash in the oldest rocks of the American continent, there stretched a thousand miles of good white pine into which the saws of Lewis Merritt might have buzzed and bitten. Starting from Ohio, that burly and industrious man might have sawed his way northward, and never have reached this outpost huddle of log huts that snuggled together to keep warm in a land where winter is like to begin in the early autumn and spring hardly peeps out before the beginning of summer.

But Lewis Merritt, in the interest of an entirely problematical bettering of the family fortune, must move a thousand miles at a jump; it was not for nothing he'd given his offspring the names of Leonidas, Cassius, Alfred, Napoleon. So here at the Head of the Lakes and the absolute end of nowhere he waited for them in October of 1856; the ship of the forgotten name wallowed and snorted and splashed her paddles as she slid past Pioneer George Stuntz's dock on Minnesota Point. Over her side the twelve-year-old exuberant Leonidas Merritt yelled, and his slow-spoken brother Alfred merely looked—at Ojibways of the band of Ne-con-dis skimming over St. Louis Bay in their birch-bark canoes, at their smoking tepees on the shore, at the frontier dandy, Edwin Hall, who gave style and tone to the new community by a red shirt with white bosom, red sash, fine boots, and broadcloth pants that were Duluth's outstanding claim to civilization.

Lewis Merritt stood waiting, a fellow with strong jaws wider than the top of his head, with dark, almost terrible eyes it was hard for ordinary folks to look into. Merritt knew nothing of iron mines, real or mythical. A man of extremes, he was filled with what any prudent man would call idiotic hopes; he was somberly enthusiastic about this country that sane men then called uninhabitable.

II

AT ONEOTA on St. Louis Bay, Merritt had pre-
empted his land, had built his log house, and it was
here the Merritt boys began their thirty-five years
of frost-nipped, black-fly bitten, lean-bellied education in hunting iron. Their front yard sloped
down into the cold river water of the St. Louis.
Their back yard sloped up into the pine woods that
covered the great hill of the Duluth gabbro. A mass
of old gray rock is this gabbro, that the wise men
say boiled up in a fearful subterranean eruption
untold millions of years ago to help make the peculiar deep hole that now holds the waters of Lake
Superior. But for the pioneer urchin, Leonidas
Merritt, the brim of this hill in his father's back
yard was the edge of nowhere, the beginning of
mystery; and even his dad couldn't say what lay
north beyond it. There were yarns, rumors young
Lon heard gravely discussed at George Stuntz's
store, of gold, of silver and copper back there—and
of course this lithe, pleasant-faced surveyor and
prince of bushwhackers, Stuntz, was by far the
best educated man at the head of the Lakes—but

who'd ever really been over the brow of the hill?

"Well," mulled Lon, "the Indians 've been there. I'll bet old Chief Loon Foot has canoed up back of that hill. . . . They say the St. Louis River flows down in big waterfalls off the back side of it. . . ."

So Leonidas Merritt became the white godson of old Loon Foot, became his great favorite, got himself adopted into the band of the Ne-con-dis, heard from the lips of that vagabondish old worthy the quasi-geological story of Nanibojou, the Great Hare, who, in the very ancient days when the waters came and covered the whole face of the country, had built a great raft and kept all the beasts and birds alive upon it. Any modern mother would have worried herself gray-headed over the tricks Loon Foot taught her young bull of the woods, Leonidas, for his education. But Hepzibeth? She had seven boys' clothes to mend and make; she was nurse to all of Oneota and Duluth; she became hotel keeper of the Head of the Lakes; when no steamboat came, and the candles began to run low, she saved grease, sixty-eight pounds of grease, and fashioned it into clumsy homemade candles, hardened with alum for lack of beeswax; and to the young pioneer women of Duluth who waited the coming of their first children—with no doctor—Hepzibeth was midwife. So Leonidas, and even ten-year-old Al-

8

fred, had plenty of rope for dangerous lessons from old Loon Foot.

"When we get a little bigger we'll paddle up behind the hill!" Leonidas—who was aggressive, obstreperous and by way of being a little of a brag-gart—told the silent Alfred. And there's Leonidas, in the years before his voice has begun to change, sitting with the ease, the balance of some young water-centaur in a birch-bark canoe that would make a careful man sit absolutely tight and part his hair in the middle to keep right side up on a millpond without a breeze. Pretty soon this wide-shouldered youngster is far up the gray river that makes its great horse-shoe curve down from the gabbro mountain; he's up where the water runs white, and roars. With a cunning dig of the paddle he sets his canoe from eddy across to dangerous eddy at the foot of a wild white rapid. Then one day he starts the sharp nose of his boat down the ominous "V" of smooth water that sucks over a brink between huge bowlders. He's lost in the spray of the boiling chute. . . . He gives a boisterous yell as his canoe bobs up and down, but still right side up, in the waves at the foot of it.

"Eh-eh! Eh-eh-eh!" old Loon Foot grunts and cackles his approval. Lon is in his riverman's apprenticeship.

While Lewis Merritt was scratching his head,

9

finding out there were too many logs to saw, and too few folks to build houses with them, and next to nobody to buy them, young Lon—Alf tagging at his heels—vanishes into the thick growth of poplars and silver birch on the low ground by the river and starts toward the giant pines up the side of the hill—

"Wonder how far we could see from the top?" Lon asks Alf. They get to the top, scratched, legs aching, and out of breath: they push ahead on level ground into a tangle of spruce, of balsam-fir, into a welter of vegetation that would lose your modern city man in a hundred yards. The sun snuffs out, under one of those sudden scudding masses of vapor that flies down Lake Superior all the way from Thunder Bay: snowflakes sift down through the evergreen bows—time to find the way home.

"No—we're all right. Home is east!" asserts the confident Lon. "Loon Foot says the big pines 'most always lean toward the rising of the sun. . . ."

"But they're every which way—" complains Alf, younger and maybe a little nervous.

"All right—but Loon Foot says trees 've always got most limbs pointing south," answers Lon. "An' look! *All* the trees 've got the most moss on *this* side—an' that means north!"

Faces red with the damp cold, feet swollen too big for their shoes, hungry as wolves for the ever-

10

lasting potatoes and whitefish of those fish and potato days of Duluth, they show up home for supper,
for a pat on the head from the extremely preoccu-
pied Hepzibeth who'll never know how near she's
come to losing them. The boys sleep in the deep
coma their education has earned them—not knowing it's their knack of going straight in the woods,
away from signposts, from section corners, from
any kind of trail, away even from water—that'll get
them their fortune way north on Mis-sa-be Wasju.

III

It wasn't only log-sawing, husky boy-begetting
visionaries like Lewis Merritt who were drawn
toward this desolation by the mystical magnet of
belief in an unknown, in an entirely theoretical
treasure back there over the gabbro hill. There was
George R. Stuntz, who'd surveyed more blank
virgin United States than any government land
surveyor that ever lived, who'd had a complete education, two whole years of it, at the Grand River
Institute in Ohio—in "mathematics, engineering,
chemistry and surveying." All of this book-learning
should have taught him the impossibility of ever
civilizing this blank map of misty muskeg, rock,
and forest. Stuntz came, along with his boss, old
Surveyor-General Sargent. He took one look at
safe, snug St. Louis Bay, walled off from the terrible Lake Superior waves by a fortunate sandspit
built up by the ages-long churning and pounding
of those billows themselves.

"I came in 1852," wrote old Stuntz, long after.
"I saw the advantages of Minnesota Point as
clearly then as I do now. I went away to make a

12

report, and returned next spring and came for good. I saw as clearly then as I do now that this was the heart of the continent commercially and so I drove my stakes."

What did Stuntz see? What could he have seen any more than Lewis Merritt saw? He could look east and see water, south and see woods, north and west and see only the blank brim of that ancient volcanic hill, terraced with by-gone shores two hundred feet higher than those of present Lake Superior, cutting a pale northern horizon into saw-teeth of pines and spruce against a light blue sky. But Stuntz had energy, was *the* man to map, measure, lay out and find out about this country. With a little ax—that now lies neglected as if it were of no significance at all, behind an office door in Duluth—he ran land lines and subdivided towns, cut the boundary posts that said here's where Minnesota stops and where Wisconsin starts. There was in him the miraculous energy of the woodsman's god, Paul Bunyan, even though he was a smallish man, and there is record that, in the lead of a little bunch of volunteers, Stuntz cut a road through thirty boggy, shin-tangled miles of alternate bush and giant pine, of hard birch and soft squaw-wood all the way from Iron River to St. Louis Bay. That was to get three yoke of oxen, a cart, and two cows—these were the absolute,

13

original, pioneer cows of the northwest country—
through to Superior and Duluth. The cows were to
give milk for the kids of frontier women who had
not even started west; the carts and oxen were de-
signed to transport unknown cargoes over the uncut
roads of this land where there was no logical reason
for transporting anything. In the woods Stuntz
worked hard, lived on pork, flour, and tea, and was
sober; back in his shack on Minnesota Point it was
his habit to relax, to get drunk, to see visions that
were all the more marvelous because they under-
valued the still unknown reality that lay hidden behind the hill.

IV

Stuntz talks in a whisper to Captain Pratt: "See here—I've got this absolutely straight. Professor Eames—you know he's our State Geologist—has just come back from a canoe trip from up Lake Vermilion way. He's been trying to keep it dark—but he's discovered gold-bearing quartz up there—"

Pratt is cynical, sententious: "Eames—how could he discover anything—why, he's only a geologist!"

"Don't talk nonsense. Our State wouldn't appoint a man to that job who didn't know iron, or copper, or gold when he saw it. Come on, Pratt—let's get our outfits ready; I know that country up north there like the palm of my hand. Come on—there's a chance he's right. And nobody has heard of it—nobody. Here's our chance to beat them to it—here's the chance *to open up this country!*"

It's the spring of 1865, and George Stuntz and Pratt are bending their backs over their paddles, bending with a perfect rhythm all day, giving the clear water of the St. Louis River short, choppy strokes of their paddle-blades till the tops of their backbones, just under their necks, are stiff, and sore. They're ahead of the bunch, of old Lewis Merritt and all the rest of the citizens of the Head of the Lakes who 've heard of Eames's gold by now, who are smearing pitch over the bottoms of their canoes, fumbling at their tumplines, patching their pack-sacks. They get up St. Louis River that's like a long, six-hundred-foot stairs of water, carrying their duffle past innumerable waterfalls. At last, by Esquagamo Lake and the Embarrass River they come to Wine Portage by the Mis-sa-be, the Height of Land—to the spot where water begins to flow north instead of south. Here they carry their canoe, their pork, flour, and tea several severe miles to Pike River that's hardly wide enough to float their birch-bark boat. They're bound for many-bayed Ona-ma-sa-ga-i-gan, for the Lake of the Beautiful Sunset.

They looked for gold, on the rocks along the shores, on increasingly disappointing islands among the three hundred and sixty-five islands of Lake Vermilion. They looked for gold and found—rocks. A day came when their sow-belly was cut to the last rind, and they reached into the emptiness of their last flour sack for a final handful of flour to fry an ultimate, indigestible, but life-sustaining dough-god. They looked for gold again. Dodging white men, they met Indians, no-good Ojibways,

16

and upon quizzing these dark-faced children of nature, received in return waves of the hand in vague directions, and sentences composed of monosyllabic grunts.

Their hope of gold began to vanish with their vanishing supply of grub. They bought fish and wild-rice from the Ojibways, and kept looking. They got thin. They jabbed holes in their belts, and tightened them back past the last hole to keep their pants from falling off, and they kept looking, and found nothing.

"God! this is a useless country," groused Captain Pratt. "What could happen here? What ever *has* happened?"

In despair they finally did talk to a white man, one who bore the now forgotten but then unique distinction of being the one white settler in the seven hundred odd miles between Duluth and Hudson Bay. He was a queer man, named North Albert Posey, who for some reason had taken it into his head that it was his mission in life to teach the Indians the art of blacksmithing. North Albert Posey said, with the hesitation of a man out of practice in speaking English:

"Well, Mr. Stuntz—there may be gold hereabouts—but I've never seen it. And the Indians haven't. But now, when it comes to iron—"

But Stuntz and Pratt had no thought of iron.

17

And they laid new plans, to sneak east—there were other white men coming—across this last bay and around that point yonder, and then up over that big jasper hill there. . . .

It's a foggy morning. They're up and away before breakfast. "I believe we've given them the slip," says Stuntz to Captain Pratt.

It was so thick ahead that Pratt in the bow could hardly see a hundred feet ahead of him, and long afterward Stuntz gave it out as his belief that Providence had sent them that fog, so that they alone might have the glory and honor of their approaching, fantastic discovery. . . .

Expertly the two of them feathered their paddles, with twists of their wrists that shot their light boat over the water with never a splash or a gurgle. "This is luck," whispered Stuntz, as they passed the mouth of Pike River close by an Indian Camp— "even those 'Jibways won't know where we're going." There is a queer exaltation about Stuntz that the cold mist can't blanket.

Poor Pratt in the bow keeps a strained look ahead over the innocent-looking surface of the smooth, brown, treacherous water, water peculiarly hard to see into, that has, in places, rocks within three inches of the surface. They are nice jagged stones sharp enough to rip the bottom out of you before you can say Jack Robinson. The canoe

18

crunches to a stop on a beach, thick with alder and little cedars; into the cover of this almost impenetrable brush they pull her, quickly knock down a couple of trees of dead, punky squaw-wood and set it ablaze with a bit of birch-bark to boil their breakfast kettle. If there is gold; today there may be gold—

"Well—anyway," smiles Stuntz as he wipes the tea out of his mustache with the back of his hand, "I bet you we've given the rest of 'em the slip."

"Oh—but what a country! What's ever goin' to happen here? What's *ever* happened here?" So growls Pratt, mock-mournfully as is permitted of a good campmate.

Of course, in the history of America, in the inconceivably vast stretch of the history of the face of the earth, the presence of these two men here was ridiculous. What *had* happened here, ever? There sat the curiously sanguine, the eternally hopeful George Stuntz—and educated, he should have known better—in the foggy, dripping bush eighty-five miles as the goose flies, north from Duluth. To the south of him there lay other lakes, separated by knee-deep muskeg swamp, until very soon you reached a line of low barren hills, ex-mountains they were, the Heights of the Mis-sa-be. These were the so-called Giant's Range—ancient mountains their Indian ex-owners had given the

19

name the white men spell "Mis-sa-bay" or "Mes-a-bi" or "Mes-a-ba." Though a tenderfoot would hardly notice those low hills now, they were named according to an ancient legend teaching that these were the grandmother hills of them all. And maybe, who knows, that legend was sound geology—for if we're to believe the theories of the wisest modern rock-readers, those rocks are as old as any you'll find on the face of the earth.

This land was eventless, useless, yes—and Stuntz was a fool for being there—maybe. Yet over there by the Mis-sa-be hills there had occurred—in the mists of millions of years ago—events most strange. Here God had caused volcanic hell to pop as he built the very backbone of the American continent. *Then* there must have been vast fireworks—with never a human eye to see them—as the rocks of the Mis-sa-be boiled up, hot, among hissing giant clouds of steam, to poke their young noses above a waste of water. What then had they brought with them out of the metal-rich heart of the earth—for man?

Stuntz tucked their pitiful, nearly empty packsacks and duffle under their overturned canoe; there was in his face a sort of idiotic determination: "If I don't find gold I'll find something."

But what could be left for Stuntz after those millions—maybe billions—of years since the young rocks had raised their heads above the water? Ages had passed, to mash them, break them, bow them queerly up into lofty mountains, in remote days when our Rockies weren't even babies. Enormously uneventful eons had gone by, and those proud mountains had been worn down to nothing by the tiny but tremendous power of wind, weather and water.

George Stuntz, himself reader of the rocks, may well have known this: that there had been strange days when the very first indication of what's now North America was this very Mis-sa-be—when Duluth, when all our fair land to the south was a waste of water with this low Mis-sa-be its northern shore.

"Ho-hum," muttered Stuntz, "let's get at it." He picked up his hammer and pick, started crashing the bush toward the jasper hill.

He had gone hardly forty rods from his canoe, when through the bush a wall of rock loomed up before him. "Here's a lead—look at this, will you!" he called to Pratt. Here was a vein of beautiful quartz better than eight feet wide, and in a moment the explorer was on to it, squinting all over it, chipping at it with his hammer, with Pratt looking eagerly over his shoulder.

"No—doesn't look like much," said Stuntz, and his eye roved back from the freshly fractured quartz in his hand to the wall of rock. "What's this funny-looking stuff on each side of the quartz vein? . . . Oh, yes, it's slate. But there's something else mixed in with it."

It was iron, impure iron, small bands of grayish iron ore between alternate stripes and bands of slate; iron of no consequence when you were looking for gold. And Stuntz started scrambling up the hill, following the lure of his vein of quartz, chipping it with his hammer, hopefully as he went up the hill, less hopefully as he threw away one piece after another, less and less hopefully as the exposure of quartz grew narrower, as the blackish gray walls of slaty iron in each side of it grew wider. Here they were at the top of the hill, and, worse luck, their quartz vein had run out entirely —but here was something Stuntz had never seen before, something outlandish. Here were immense rocks, mottled and banded with a curious green and gray and reddish black—

"Here, Pratt! Just heft this once!" and Stuntz put in his partner's hand a chunk of rock that was curiously, unexpectedly heavy.

Excited, Stuntz let himself down the steep south face of the mountain, looking, peering. Where was the slate now? The slate had run out, as the quartz had done. He swung at the face of the weird-looking rock—it was a huge gray-black cliff—with his little pick.

"Here, pard—just heft *this* one!" shouted Stuntz.

He tossed to Pratt a chunk of stuff five times the weight of any ordinary rock, terrifically ponderous, so amazingly heavy it slipped through Pratt's surprised hands. The freshly broken surface of this newly discovered piece of the northern land was hard, was grayish, and it gleamed with innumerable points that flashed like tiny diamonds. It was hematite—as near as you could get pure hematite, high grade iron ore that came, years after, to be yelled for by the down-lakes furnace men, to be called "Minnesota, No. 1, Bessemer," to be prized as millers prize Minnesota No. 1, Hard Wheat.

Who had ever seen the like of it? And George Stuntz cocked his rock-reader's head proudly at his marvelous cliff of pure iron ore, that stood out there so strangely naked, left there for the first bush-whacker to see, by an erratically beneficent Nature, a Nature that likes to hide her treasures. Stuntz followed the great twenty-five-foot-wide streak of this grand ore down the mountain. How easy it had been. All he'd had to do had been to be the first to get to this spot—and look. So George Stuntz the gold-hunter found iron, iron that is common as mud, that's unspectacular, that's more staple than wheat, because, as the great iron hunter Osborn says, there's absolutely no substitute for it. It was part of that iron which was to help build today's fantastic age of steel.

So the explorer Stuntz discovered the Vermilion Iron Range—twenty years before it was needed.

V

LEWIS HOWELL MERRITT came back from the fizzled-out gold rush on Lake Vermilion, not one bit discouraged about that water-logged, bleak plain up there over the hill's brim. No matter how many prospectors had been swallowed up in those terrible feather-bed swamps, no matter that he himself had waked up, shivering under summer blankets on a morning in July, maybe to find a quarter of an inch of ice at the lake's edge—it was a grand country! Lewis knew about the iron; everybody knew about the iron. For, in spite of Stuntz's precautions to sneak away through the fog while he was looking for gold, this was only a sort of hide-and-go-seek game of that open-hearted pioneer. Stuntz was never a fellow to play his cards close to his chest and he told Lewis Merritt, or anybody who wanted to know, about his marvelous mountain of iron. And when hot toddies had warmed him on a cold Sunday afternoon, when he was relaxing after his leg-weary, half-starved searching, George Stuntz had become oracular:

"When this country is developed, that big moun-

tain of iron will do it. When they get to hauling
that iron out, they will bring its supplies in cheap,"
so George told the boys.

Lewis Merritt, a terrific Methodist, you may
guess didn't hold with George Stuntz's sprees, not
a bit of it; but he knew as well as anybody else that
the surveyor was the Nestor of all Northwest explorers, was absolutely reliable. Then too Lewis
had talked to North Albert Posey—who Stuntz
was the first to admit had known about the iron
long before he himself had. Again, old Lewis had
made a curious find of his own. On his way home,
as he came through the tangle of rocks, lakes, bogs
and morasses that lay round Birch Lake on the east
end of the Mis-sa-be hills, Lewis himself had picked
up rocks. It was a bewildering country, where his
compass needle had whirled round, gone suddenly
crazy on him. It was country like to lose a man,
drive him frantic, starve him to death before he
could get himself straightened out. It was be-
witched.

Here Lewis had picked up a rock, and had stood,
lost in new wool-gathering notions, looking west
down those Mis-sa-be hills.

He came back to Oneota a changed man. Yes—
these first ten fish-and-potato years had been tough.
But now there was a reason for his having lugged
poor Hepzibeth and all their kids up here, and it

wasn't after all for nothing that they'd near froze, half-starved. Lewis straightened his shoulders, came back to Hepzibeth with a new explanation, that was more than an excuse, for his being a rover born. There was iron!

The Civil War was over, and presently the huskiest, wildest-dreaming of the eight Merritt boys, the broad-shouldered bucko, Leonidas, came back from it. Lewis Merritt, who had waited for this event, gathered his boys round him in the light of the fire, in the little log house by the cold profitless river in Oneota.

"Boys—I've got something to tell you," and the thin-lipped, fierce-eyed man, already a patriarch though still too young for it, cleared his throat and he looked at Leonidas.

Lewis knew that this young worthy, though only twenty-two and fourth in line of Hepzibeth's sons, was the leader of this band of brothers. Lon had walked, packing his own grub, over next to no roads at all, over one hundred and fifty miles from Duluth to St. Paul to enlist "for the duration" in Brackett's Cavalry Battalion. He'd had his picture taken armed to the teeth with a carbine, a sword, and an enormous revolver stuck in his belt, in front. For two years he'd ranged the Dakotas, fought the Sioux, caught typhoid fever and been left for dead by panic-stricken pals; but nothing could down

him, and he'd wormed, sneaked, and fought his
way, alone, through gangs of hostile Indians to re-
join his command. He was rough as hemlock and
tough as hickory. Here he was back, raring to go
as the saying goes, ready to open up the country.

"Boys," boomed old Lewis, "you that are voy-
agers, I've been up north—way back of the Mis-
sa-be hills to Lake Vermilion, and there's wealth
up there this whole nation ain't dreamed of—"

Lon's dark eyes flared; he adored old Lewis,
though fearing him thoroughly as the rest of the
boys feared him. He absolutely believed him. He
had to, for with this father there was no monkey
business, there was nothing whatever modern about
him.

"I tell you there's iron up there worth more than
all the gold in California!" He told them a circum-
stantial story of Indian yarns about iron hills and
rivers that ran red, of North Albert Posey, and of
the mountain of iron George Stuntz had discovered
up by Lake Vermilion. He rose. He stalked to a
cupboard and opened a drawer. He brought out a
chunk of multi-colored, strangely banded rock that
glittered in the light of the flaming birch logs.

"This comes from near Birch Lake, up on the
east end of the Mis-sa-be hills." Lon's eyes gleamed
—for how could he know this was only a piece of
low-grade magnetite, lean in iron, of no value as
ore?

28

"Now mark my words—Stuntz hasn't found *anything* yet by Vermilion Lake, compared to—" and Lewis swept his arm back toward the north, in an enormous arc.

"Compared to what's there—what's hidden there. There's *bound* to be iron all the way along those Mis-sa-be hills—way west from Birch Lake—all the way to Grand Rapids, you know that new lumber town, with all the saloons, on the Mississippi. Now I've formed a theory about it—" and the stern man eloquently turned his theory into fact: "the Mis-sa-be is an iron range—rich, rich, rich in iron!"

Hepzibeth sat to one side, knitting, her face inscrutable, unenthusiastic. But Hepzibeth didn't complain.

"Yes, dad!" cried Lon, starting up.

"When you get the chance, I'm asking you to take a look for this iron I know is in the Mis-sa-be hills."

So Lewis Merritt sowed the seed for what turned out to be for twenty years a wild-goose chase for his boys, an intermittent, grim and disappointing hunt—that ended amazingly, at last, in two years of triumph, and tragedy, for them in the early nineties, and in the revolution of the United States steel industry.

VI

GEORGE STUNTZ went east to tell the amazing treasure he'd found, and surely it couldn't be that he was too far ahead of the times. Six years before, the blast furnaces and rolling mills down by the Allegheny had begun literally to suck the red ore down the lakeways from Lake Superior's iron rim. Hungry for iron to smelt into cannon to free the slaves, the Pennsylvania forges were blasting better than 200,000 tons of dusty red rocks from the Marquette iron range on the south shore of Lake Superior in 1864. The cheerful, cherubic, and subsequently philanthropic Andrew Carnegie was just finding out how gloriously profitable it was to smelt pig iron into cannons—or anything else. By a chance called in to allay a quarrel in their company, he bought in with that blacksmith genius, Andrew Kloman, and his beer-drinking brother, Anton— who were famous for forging the very best wrought-iron axles in America. Carnegie saw how they'd expanded in a few years from their little forge and their single wooden trip-hammer in a basement down by Girty's Run in Allegheny. His canny eyes

looked round him, saw America's hunger, her absolute need for bands of iron, for a framework of iron
to stiffen her huge sprawling weakness. Carnegie
looked south, and saw torn roadbeds, ripped up on
Sherman's hell-roaring march to the sea—new rails
would now have to be laid down there. In the Mid-
West two parallel threads of iron were crawling
toward the sunset over the right-of-way of the new
Union Pacific. From the lower corner of Lake
Michigan railroads were starting in all directions
like great spokes, growing out from a new hub,
Chicago—and they ran over prairies whose tough
black sod called for plows of the finest iron, made
from stuff stronger than iron—to prepare them for
the sowing of the maize.

George R. Stuntz traveled to Astoria, Long
Island, to see his old boss, General Sargent, with
a vision of the future of his bleak country that was
certainly not surpassed by that of Jim Hill himself, and with a knowledge of it that was equaled
by nobody else at all. Stuntz was a most curious
observer, part poetic, part matter-of-fact, part scientific.* He was forever vanishing from his little
trading post on Minnesota Point to range up and
down Lake Superior's shores. It was this store-
keeper who first noted the queer fact that the north
rocky shore of the great lake had recently risen,

* See Appendix A, page 217.

and that its gentler south shore had recently over-
flowed. He was always dreaming about this ominous news that the whole deep-gouged basin of
Lake Superior, the whole northern land was tilting,
was warping downward toward the southwest, upward toward the northeast. To the north and east
he'd seen, and sketched, old shore lines of the lake
rising eastward out of the water, and on this shore,
rivers cascaded into the lake without any harbors
at all. To the south and west he saw that the slowly
sinking shore was backing the lake up into the
rivers—and to this tilting, before which men must
stand so utterly helpless, Stuntz believed his own
beloved St. Louis Bay was due.

He even wrote a short, elegantly worded paper
about it, and this treatise was published in the Proceedings of the American Academy of Sciences, in
1870. Is it a wonder George Stuntz never made
money?

In Astoria, he told General Sargent of the perfect harbor of Duluth, of the dark soil so fit for
grain, that lay behind it a thousand miles toward
the west. "General—that grain's simply *got* to go
east through Duluth—it's going to be the cheapest
way, it's the most natural!"

Then there was the Lake, always the Lake—
31,200 square miles of cold pure water in Lake
Superior from which to net untold tons of the finest

trout, the sweetest whitefish; and there were ten thousand inland lakes back of Duluth from which to snare vast harvests of pike, of bass, of muskellunge.

"And, General—those stories of minerals aren't dreams any more. I've myself discovered a mountain of iron—high grade ore—up by Lake Vermilion; it's got to go down by the lakes to be used —it must go by Duluth."

What a man, this George Stuntz, with a fanatic's impersonal, selfless enthusiasm, but still exact, reliable. Next year General Sargent moved his family to Duluth and began to build hotels.

Stuntz left never a stone unturned, never missed a bet, but went with a letter to the optimistic capitalist, Jay Cooke of Philadelphia—this was the man who'd financed the North through the Civil War to the tune of better than two billions of dollars—no less. Stuntz spoke his piece. Jay Cooke, too, came west, was rowed from Superior across St. Louis Bay by a young boy in a boat, and upon reaching the Minnesota shore, took off his plug hat, and in a fiery speech told a chance band of Chippewas who he was, and what now was to be the future of this their former country. The Indians admired the tall, bearded financier vastly, but didn't understand what he said. He gave them all brand-new twenty-five-cent pieces, then with the

white worthies of Duluth he agreed to float the
bonds of the proposed Lake Superior and Mississippi railway—and returned forthwith to Philadelphia. So the northwest was opened at last; at last
there was capital here: and what do the efforts of
bushwhackers, land-lookers, explorers, avail—even
when they're inspired bushwhackers like Stuntz
and the Merritts—without capital?

So Jay Cooke really started the growth of the
up till then almost completely useless, foolish little
city founded by those penniless pioneers. Realtors
bought, sold, and flourished; saloons—which later
became esthetic with gorgeous geraniums in their
windows—increased in numbers. Lewis Merritt
caught the fever and built a hotel of his own in
Oneota; it was strictly temperance, substantial, of
two stories with a long porch, and surmounted by
a handsome cupola with windows from which the
Bay might be viewed.

In a glow—and justifiably a little bit proud—
Stuntz like a beaver plunged into what was his
grandest work, aside from the discovery of iron by
Lake Vermilion. General Warren offered him the
position of Captain, to expend all of $10,000, to
build the road to Vermilion Lake. The year before,
he'd located it—and who except Stuntz could have
laid out such an easy way, slanting up to the brim
of the great gabbro hill, then striking north,
through a succession of white pine forests, vast

"I SAW AS CLEARLY THEN AS I DO NOW THAT THIS WAS THE
HEART OF THE CONTINENT"

"AT LAST EVEN LEWIS MERRITT WENT, TAKING HEPZIBETH,
WHO DIDN'T COMPLAIN"

tracts of treacherous muskeg, across embarrassing little rivers like the Cloquet, like the Whiteface, that meandered westward through morasses until they fell by pretty but useless waterfalls and rapids into the St. Louis on its way to Lake Superior. "The bowlders were so thick," remarked Stuntz, long after, "that you couldn't drive a team at all without moving them out of the way."

From July 1st until December 10th Stuntz worked, with eighteen men, two ox-teams and wagons. In that time he finished the eighty-four miles of the Vermilion Trail from Duluth to Ona-ma-sa-ga-i-gan. It was a road good enough to haul supplies in—even in the summer!

Then, in 1873, the banking house of Jay Cooke blew up with a tragic bang; the Menominee and Gogebic iron ranges were discovered down below in Michigan and there was too much iron; the population of Duluth melted away from six thousand to a scant three. At last even Lewis Merritt went, taking Hepzibeth, who didn't complain, and didn't forget her knitting. Lewis Merritt hadn't lost an iota of his faith in the north country, but at sixty-odd, seven months of winter doesn't seem—well, doesn't seem so bracing, maybe. And surely he had earned the right to work his last years in the sunshine. So they settled on a farm in Missouri, where the robins come early and the redbirds sing on bright days, even in the winter.

35

VII

But the boys stuck. ". . . We were not discouraged," wrote Leonidas, "and managed to get through the winters comfortably, and at each succeeding spring we whistled with the blackbirds and sang with the robins, because we knew ere long that the world's homeless hosts would file past our doors to take possession of a smiling land." In that land that smiles—sometimes—Leonidas, Alfred, and their adolescent brother Cassius did everything. While Lon was still fighting the ungrateful Sioux in the Dakotas, Alfred shipped before the mast on the schooner *Pierpont,* bound with iron ore down the Lakes from Marquette to Cleveland. Alf was sober, utterly dependable, oblivious to shipmates whom the poetic Leonidas would have cottoned to or fought with. These sailors were wild, forgotten swashbucklers who later bawled:

"Some sailors took shovels while others got spades,
 And some took wheelbarrows, each man to his
    trade.
We looked like red devils, our fingers got sore,
We cursed Escanaba and that damned iron ore."

36

Alf was simply a man to see that the iron ore got safely down the lakes. He coasted past the mysterious pictured sandstone rocks east of Marquette, and it would have aroused no awestruck nor poetic thoughts in Alf if he'd known that the bottom of Lake Superior lay four hundred feet below the level of the sea. Nor would he have speculated on the unknown force that had opened up this rift in the earth's face—millions of years before the ice cap had come down from the north. But Alf learned to box the compass.

Captain Beebe could trust Wheelsman Alfred Merritt to get his precious *Pierpont* down snag-infested St. Mary's River, and past the rocks near *Zheshebe Minis* where the world-famous iron-hunter, Chase Osborn, now makes camp and brews new and wise philosophies. Wheelsman Merritt didn't know of the Great Freeze that had happened thousands of years ago before there were any Great Lakes at all. He stood at the helm, on the poop of that absurd little iron-ore schooner, as she nosed out past Drummond Island and Point Détour into Lake Huron—and he'd never heard of the giant fingers of the Continental Glacier, the mysterious ice cap, thousands of feet thick, that had once stretched southward, later to melt and make Lake Huron possible. So prosaic was Alf, that he'd have hardly opened his eyes, squinting from behind narrow, observant slits, if you'd told him of the ancient, maybe pre-human, epic thaw that had then followed, driving those ice fingers slowly, slowly back into the north. He would have kept busy learning the knack of coiling rope on the deck, as he heard how those disappearing lobes of ice had left ice-dammed ponds at their southern edges, desolate sheets of cold gray water without life, that grew into Lakes Erie and Huron on the east, and sky-blue Michigan on the west, as the giant melt continued. Alfred Merritt was the man the hard-cursing Captain Beebe liked to have at the wheel when the *Pierpont,* near to bursting with heavy red ore, wallowed down Lake Huron before a northeast gale that chased ominous squalls of snow ahead of it.

Of certain fortunate successions of events in the Great Lakes' infinitely gradual shrinking, this embryo iron-man, Merritt, never knew: how the water of these immense pre-historic seas had once covered completely the very iron he was taking down to Cleveland; how the water of all the lakes had once swirled southwestward into the Mississippi over present Chicago; how all their water had once boiled down the Mohawk into the Hudson before there was a Niagara Falls. But Alfred Merritt did sense this, being an extremely practical man: that this stretch of water was a mighty convenient

way to get the red ore from the top of the lakes
down to where there were enough farms, factories,
furnaces to use it. And he surreptitiously smiled
at Captain Beebe, who swore vast forgotten Great
Lakes cusswords, because he was getting only seven
dollars and a quarter a ton for carrying 270 tons of
iron to Cleveland, on his little windjammer that
would take nine years to move one cargo of a modern ore-boat.

Leonidas and Alfred did everything, and without knowing it got to know this northwest land that
was never wet enough, raw enough, cold enough to
seem dismal to them. In the late sixties they learned
surveying, by getting jobs as chainmen on Jay
Cooke's Lake Superior and Mississippi railroad.
With their own hands they laid the keel of the first
ship ever built at the Head of the Lakes. She was
67 feet over all and of 69 tons burthen; they named
her *Chaska;* they carried stones in her from Bass-
wood Island to the new Government piers at
Ontonagon; in a northeast gale that howled across
the Lake from off the Height of Land they piled
their *Chaska* up on the rocks, were maybe saved
from pneumonia by an Ontonagon saloonkeeper
who gave them dry clothes and hot food. They were
$1,500 in debt and chopped wood in the bush north
of Duluth until they'd got enough money to pay
off every cent of it. Then they built a new schooner,

the *Handy,* and traded up and down Lake Superior until they knew every cranny of her 1,500 miles of coast line, from Two Harbors east to Batchawanna Bay and back along the south shore to Duluth.

They learned everything excepting iron and the art of iron-mining; to make ends meet they worked one on each end of a crosscut saw in winter, their bodies wringing wet with sweat while their noses were nipped by frosts of thirty degrees below zero. In the summer they were off over the hill's brim toward the Mis-sa-be, learning the now nearly forgotten art of land-looking. Leonidas—who was always too confident—was proud of the way he could push his squat, broad-shouldered five-feet-eight-inches through tangles of balsam, spruce, and alder underbrush, far away from guiding watercourses, altogether too far away from his birch-bark boat that was his only means of getting back alive from this forbidding country. Alfred and Lon could both look up the trunk of a giant pine and make a shrewd guess at how many feet of lumber you'd saw out of it. Both of them were cunning at running a compass, far away from any trail, among rocks that mysteriously caused the needle to point in almost any direction except north. They married. Hopefully they begat children, who were like as not to be born while their fathers were away—unheard from—on months-long cruises in the bush.

Leonidas and Alfred remembered old Lewis Merritt's prophecy: "The iron mines up under the Mis-sa-be will be worth all the gold in California." They voyaged the Mis-sa-be Heights from end to end. They saw never a hint of iron.

VIII

MANY houses in Duluth were empty in 1875; many others, tenanted by gloomy settlers, had socks and old shirts stuck in broken window panes—and what good were these to keep the raw wind off Kitchi Gammi from howling through? Duluth looked like any other forlorn hope; looked like anything but "the commercial heart of the continent." But George R. Stuntz was up over the gabbro hill once more, up Lake Vermilion way, and this time things were really going to happen. Capital, and very important eastern capital, had heard of his iron. At last—

For who was with Stuntz but Professor Chester, from Hamilton College in New York State? Chester was a distinguished geologist, an authority on mines, a true expert on many things mineral. The genial Professor sat in Stuntz's canoe, brushed the black-flies out of his whiskers, smacked the venomous mosquitoes on the back of his neck, and bravely didn't complain. Important matters were afoot; far-reaching plans were astir in the financial brains of Philadelphia; it wasn't to formulate some scientific theory about how many billions of years old this backbone of the American continent might be, that Professor Chester was being paddled north by Stuntz. Charlemagne Tower the elder had sent him north to report, yes or no, about commercially profitable iron deposits in northern Minnesota.

It was a confusion of rumor and fact that had stirred the imagination of Chester's boss, this banker who was so appropriately named Charlemagne. Tower looked like a Charlemagne; he had eyes that meant no monkey business, had a rank, lush growth of white beard and sweeping mustache that coalesced, so that you couldn't tell at all where the mustache left off and the beard began—it was a magnificent growth that must have made his bold words come out thickly, that must have made eating an adventure. Tower had this useful characteristic, without which all the bushwhacking of Stuntz, Lewis Merritt, and his seven iron sons and grandsons would have meant nothing: he was bullish on the supposed enormous resources and conjectural future wealth and prosperity of our American land. He sat back in Philadelphia and knew there must be plenty of iron—somewhere; and he had faith that America was full of men who could find it. Charlemagne had heard a confusion of reports about this new northern Minnesota region; the old Ontonagon rumor of the twelve-mile-long hill of iron on the Mis-sa-be Heights had reached him. Then too, some lean magnetic ore, dug out of the eastern Mis-sa-be in 1875 by Peter Mitchell, the explorer, had been analyzed by Chester. "Maybe not commercially valuable," had come the report, "but it certainly justifies exploring these Mis-sa-be Heights."

But most important of all, a bright New Englander, an enthusiastic go-getting promoter named George C. Stone, a plump-cheeked, hopeful man with full lips, close-cropped mustache and a beard that was more restrained, less tropical, than Tower's, had got George Stuntz to bring fifty pounds of iron back in his pack-sack from his iron mountain by the shore of Lake Vermilion.

"And that ore really made the geologists in the east sit up and take notice," said Stuntz.

So here stood Stuntz and Professor Chester on the shores of Ona-ma-sa-ga-i-gan, where once Stuntz had foolishly looked for gold. We must certainly admire the good sense of Charlemagne, or George C. Stone, or the professor himself, for having picked out George Stuntz for guide. It would have been rash, not to say positively foolhardy, for the professor to have ventured alone, or with any ordinary cruisers picked up in Duluth at random, among the confusing bays and compass-bewitched shores of Lake Vermilion. Chester was undisputably a shark on rocks, but which of the billion bowlders, crags, and looming monadnocks of this watery desolation contained the iron? Stuntz was paid, so legend has it, the excellent salary of eight dollars a day for taking Chester to this certain spot where he could say yes or no.

"It was a magnificent sight," wrote the Professor long afterward. "One exposure of ore was a natural break in a vertical bed of ore, which was at that point about twenty-five feet wide, so that it showed a solid cliff of pure hematite of that width—standing at least thirty feet out of the ground, and with large blocks of the same rich ore scattered in profusion over the ground at the foot of the cliff. . . ."

What could have been more easy to see—once you were led to it?

There was never a doubt the Professor could say yes to Charlemagne. And he went on: "Nature had here done the mining, and it was only necessary to break up the large blocks to have many tons of the finest iron ore ready for shipment when the railroad should come."

"Now they'll be able to haul supplies in here cheap!" said Stuntz, aglow at the opening up of his beloved land.

But what about the Mis-sa-be range, the alleged, reputed twelve-miles-long hill of iron the Ontonagon people were sure lay along Mis-sa-be Wasju?

The Vermilion iron that Stuntz had shown Chester was a bonanza, but not twelve miles of it, not by a long shot: and that was what Charlemagne Tower and George Stone were dreaming of. Here they were at Lake Vermilion, and they'd had to go across Mis-sa-be to get there. The Professor had had to bank on Stuntz; the Professor was certainly a man to know truth when he saw it, he only required to be taken to where truth might be found. Chester did trust Stuntz, as who wouldn't have; *he'd* voyaged across those low hills fifty times; and the explorer, with his peculiar, extremely light gray prospector's eye, with his utterly simple ideas of honesty and honor, would have taken his learned companion straight to the fabled iron hill of the Mis-sa-be if he'd known where to look for it. And finally, with that longish, inquisitive nose of his, you'd swear he'd have smelled out that iron—if by any chance it really existed.

They did scout around in the bogs and the thickets—trackless tangles they were—of what are now Town 59, Range 14, and Town 60, Range 13, of St. Louis County. They did spy lean outcrops of iron-bearing rock—magnetite; it was the same banded stuff, a kind of layer-cake of lean iron and multi-colored jasper, that Lewis Merritt had gotten unjustifiably excited about south of Birch Lake in the gold-rush days of '65. The Professor was conscientious, had the veteran land-looker take him wherever they could possibly get, *by water,* in that fly-bitten soggy eastern end of these low grand-mother hills of the Ojibways. Chester must be re-membered for his earnest scanning of this land where mosquitoes mat your neck till you're frantic, from five until seven in the morning and from six until eight at night and where the black-flies work the midday shift. Like all hunters for truth or gold, they fairly brushed by fantastic, unimaginable surprises as their canoes floated them serenely down the Embarrass River, through Embarrass Lake and across the brown still water of Lake Esqua-gamo. If they'd only crouched, crashed, broken, and fought their way through the bush, for a couple of hours, toward the west, they'd have got to that enchanted spot which later became famous as Bi-wabik—the old-timers now pronounce it peculiarly, By-wabik, with a heavy accent on the By, and snap the last two syllables off short.

"It's probably only a story," said Stuntz. "There are plenty of arm-chair prospectors." He pulled reflectively at his splendid walrus mustache as he reviewed thirty years of unfortunately unfounded rumors about his beloved north country.

"Oh—but our locations up by Lake Vermilion are enough," said the Professor. "They are excel-lent, will open up the country."

Who can blame them for not going toward what's now Biwabik? How many cruisers ever ventured far, in that utterly trackless jungle, away from the water that would surely float them back to Duluth? They did look west, as they boiled their kettle for the bitter, good dark tea on the bank at noontime. They saw nothing but stubby-topped spruce, or spire-like balsam-fir, or in the soggy places dense crowds of gently, delicately tapering tamaracks, getting ready to turn to their lovely, old-gold color of early autumn. From the top of a bowlder they could look west and see only a limitless green sea of trees, millions of them straight as pillars in cathedrals, their branches broad half-way up, and tapering toward the top to make them look like so many millions of fantastic steeples. But among them Stuntz knew there were thousands of white pine trees, down in windfalls that it would near break the best cruiser's heart to climb over; he recognized that Professor Chester was a good man, a brave one, but, alas, his whole career as a mineral expert had cultivated his mind, his intellect—at the expense of the humbler matters of his wind, and the muscles of his back and the tendons of his legs. Stuntz himself? His mustache was graying. He was still mighty tough. He was fifty-five. At that age a cruiser begins to be likely to go—where he has to. . . .

48

They passed by the Mis-sa-be.

Now things really did happen, that is, within five years they began to happen, as more iron, always more and more red ore was wanted down below at the furnaces. Who was as proud, and as absolutely indispensable as George R. Stuntz? Out of the cobwebs came his compasses, his chains, his transits once more, to survey all the country round Lake Vermilion, to plot the land where he'd discovered the iron, and thousands of acres roundabout where there *might* be iron—so that George C. Stone and Charlemagne Tower could take it up. It is a matter of history that the astute Charlemagne, what with Sioux half-breed scrip—that entitled the claimant to anything except mineral land—what with obliging entry-men, "who took up farms on barren rocks and commuted them at $1.25 an acre with a minimum of time and easy swearing"—acquired seventeen thousand acres of rich mineral land for only $40,000! In every way Stuntz was incredibly convenient. He hauled in supplies over the old Vermilion Trail he himself had built, and in March, mind you, he got in provisions for four months' living for twenty men, along with buckets and windlasses, and plenty of dynamite. He took Professor Chester back up there and showed him where to give his okay to new veins of iron-ore; he located the Duluth and Iron Range Railroad, by

49

easy grades down towards Lake Superior, across roadless lands whose secrets he was the one man to know. This was perhaps his most severe disappointment, because the road didn't carry the iron to his beloved Duluth. Charlemagne Tower had a duty to his investors and to his own pocketbook. There were solemn confabulations at which this question was asked:

"What is absolutely the cheapest, most direct way to get our iron from Vermilion to Lake Superior, Mr. Stuntz?"

As a consequence of Stuntz's honest answer, the Iron Range road ran from Vermilion not to Duluth, but to Two Harbors, twenty-five miles up the Lake.

But Stuntz's prophecies began to come true. At Ona-ma-sa-ga-i-gan, the beautiful sunsets were still more red with the red dust of iron ore. Dull explosions shook the ancient rocks harder than ever they'd been jarred since they were born in fire and bowed up into mountains. Shafts went down; houses shot up; in Surveyed Township 62 North of Range 15, West of the Fourth Principal Meridian of Minnesota, the town of Tower was born, named after Charlemagne. That was fair, and fitting, for, as one historian says:

"The energy and enterprise obviously incidental to pioneering the development of iron ore resources

50

DOMINION

MATTAWIN
DISTRICT

ANIMIKIE
DIST.

Rainy River

Lake Vermillion

VERMILLION
DISTRICT

Tower

Mountain Iron

MISSABE RANGE

LAKE SUPERIOR

Grand Rapids

Two Harbors

Duluth

St. Louis River

Here the Sons of Lewis Merritt uncovered the mighty Basins of Iron hiding at the Foot of the Missabe Hills

MARQUETTE
DISTRICT

Marquette

CRYSTAL FALLS
DIST.

PENOKEE GOGEBIC
DISTRICT

Menominee

MENOMINEE
DIST.

Mississippi

St. Croix River

Chippewa River

Wisconsin River

Green Bay

LAKE MICHIGAN

Minneapolis

St. Paul

River

W I S C O N S I N

Lake Winnebago

This is the STAGE on which was played the TRAGI-COMICAL DRAMA of the Rise & Fall of the SEVEN IRON MEN

Milwaukee

I   O   W   A

Mississippi River

Rock River

Chicago

Minnesota

M I N N E S O T A

I L L I N O I S

IND

(Rails and plows of finest iron were needed in this new country)

of Minnesota and the necessary means of transportation, first and above all is and must always be a tribute to George C. Stone and Charlemagne Tower."

From first to last these adventurers had risked three million, five hundred thousand dollars to get out Stuntz's iron. And at the new town of Tower there are manifestations of terrific energy. Red-faced, red-handed anonymous men whose clothes are covered with a dust of red, are shouting: "This is a grand country," and so they echo old Lewis Merritt. They don't care about the uncertain, feeble summers, the foggy falls, and the laggard springs when even the red-winged blackbirds look bedraggled and the robins are too cold to carol. In the winter, the company clerk writes:

"Send us a six-foot thermometer, with the zero at the top, so we can really tell how cold it gets in this here country."

They get out the iron.

George Stuntz very properly fades from this story; about him there can be no regrets. It is not clear why he never received a one-quarter interest in the new iron mines—though he could have stipulated for such a share: it was his explorer's due by the tradition of the north. Maybe it was because of a sort of lordly, slightly contemptuous pleasure that this strange man had, to scatter his discoveries about him as a kind of largesse, as he grew exultant in his cups, upon his return to Duluth, from his lonely trials and dangers. Again it is possible that Stuntz—content with his excellent pay of eight dollars a day—had a mere philosopher's negligence about the perils of a destitute old age. The records that remain show he was most interested of all in certain gigantic, prehistoric Indian mounds that he himself had discovered on the south side of Lake Esquagamo.* He was never through talking about how marvelously the Embarrass River, near Mis-sa-be Heights, had been impounded for the iron-hunting canoe-man's convenience—not by the continental ice-cap, but by the hands of ancient men.

Stuntz died stone broke, but he does have monuments: on Lake Vermilion the misty water that he crossed on that memorable morning in '65 is now called Stuntz's Bay; below the Mis-sa-be there's Stuntz Township; in geological monographs you read of a kind of ancient rock called the Stuntz Conglomerate.

Best of all there's his own road, the old Vermilion Trail—most important of all because of its enormous usefulness to America. Up this wretched, this entirely abominable tote road—which is for all that a road—a new generation of bushwhackers now begins to swarm, toward the mysterious Mis-sa-be

* See Appendix B, page 219.

hills. Down below, Captain Bill Jones and his cheerful, grimy men are making Andrew Carnegie rich; the Pittsburgh iron-masters are naming new blast furnaces, tremendous and insatiable for the red ore, "Lucy" and "Isabella"—after their good wives. When Lucy, in the midst of her desperate race to smelt more pig-iron than Isabella, catches a chill, her hard-boiled master, Skelding, shoots the cold slag out of Lucy with a cannon. Long ago the sweating workmen have thrown up their caps and, forgetting their sore backs, have yelled a wild hoorah on the first day the Lucy furnace spits out better than a hundred tons of molten iron. America is young; America is an iron-hungry Gargantua. Up Stuntz's road, the Vermilion Trail, toward their father Lewis's Mis-sa-be, grunting, swearing, singing—with hundred-pound packs on their backs— walk Leonidas, Alfred, and young Cassius Merritt.

PART TWO

ALLEGRO

"With six men and three dog trains—toboggans —we went by way of Pike River and across Rice Lake, and we were the dogs."

I

"When you're lost in the woods, my boy—when you *know* you're lost—"

The words of his Uncle Leonidas began to drift through young John E. Merritt's muddled head, and he stopped in his tracks, and wiped the sweat from his forehead. He tried to straighten the tremble out of his knees. Uncle Lon had always said, if a fellow got lost in this country—

It was November of 1884 in the depths of the Mis-sa-be woods; it was past the middle of the afternoon; daylight was turning to dark gray, and there was no sun. Flakes of snow began to sift through the pine boughs. "When you find you're lost, don't go thrashing around and crashing through the bush like a crazy moose, Johnnie—" so Leonidas Merritt had told him.

Johnnie looked down at his lumberjack's shirt—half torn off him—and at his hands scratched by brambles: here he'd been charging through the underbrush, tripping over low windfalls, running, as if death itself were after him. He wiped his forehead. "Don't fight the bush. You can't *run* away

57

from it. Just take it easy. Knock down some dead wood, some squaw-wood, an' get yourself a nice fire—" So Uncle Lon.

"Funny how I'm sweatin' this way—cold," mumbled John E., and he shivered, and felt a strange limp tiredness. It was almost dark now, and the snow was falling much thicker. But now, with scared fingers, and after having broken an entirely unsafe number of match sticks, he did get little hopeful blue and yellow flames to licking up through his pile of twigs. "When you absolutely don't know where you're at," Uncle Lon had growled through his walrus mustache:

"Get out your pipe, fill her right up to the top, sit yourself down on a log with your back to a tree in front of your fire, and smoke that pipe right down to the strong stuff in the bottom before you stir—then you'll know what to do!"

The smoke of the powerful plug tobacco tasted good in John's dry mouth; the flames popped and crackled through his bonfire of dead poplar trunks and drove the shadows back into the bush, and the heat felt good on the front of him—though his back still shivered, damply. The descending snowflakes melted in the flames; ordered thoughts began to come back into his head that half an hour ago had held only a blur, a confused, horrible tangle of trees, of imaginary trails that all led to the same

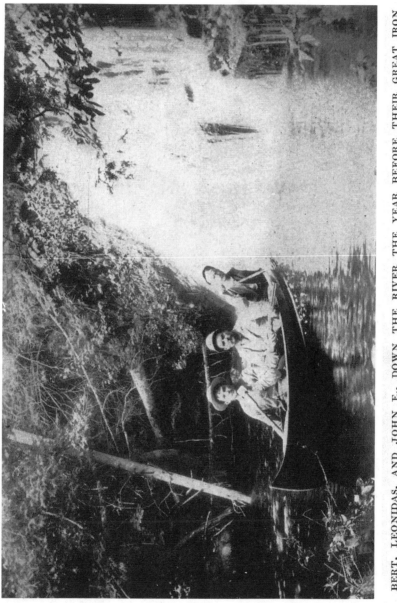

BERT, LEONIDAS, AND JOHN E., DOWN THE RIVER THE YEAR BEFORE THEIR GREAT IRON DISCOVERY ON THE MISSABE

"WHEN YOU'RE LOST IN THE WOODS, JOHNNIE——" PHOTOGRAPH OF LEONIDAS, BERT, AND JOHN E., IN CAMP, 1889

spot—nowhere. The world had been a mixed-up puzzle of low branches, lopped-off limbs, bushes that all looked exactly alike. Ahead had looked exactly like behind—and which was ahead and which behind?

John puffed blue smoke toward the draft of his fire—it was big now, and cheerful, and very safe. He made a try at a smile as he thought of the confident way he'd left his uncles, Cassius and Lewis J. Merritt, in camp that morning. With his good compass in front of him he'd started, just to look at a piece of pine, to pace off the right distance till he should meet a diagonal trail. "I'll meet you this afternoon where you'll intersect that trail," Uncle Cashie had told him. Nothing to it—who in Minnesota was a woodsman to compare with Cassius Merritt, younger brother of Alf and Leonidas? Cashie never went wrong. So John E. had started out counting his paces, squinting up monotonous successions of straight white pine trees and multiplying the feet of wood he thought might be in each one by the number of trees he'd counted, making his minits, never forgetting his number of carefully-stepped paces, watching his compass—it was a simple, if lonely science. And then his compass had started to act up—

That nervous needle began to point in any direction except north; the sun went under; and when

he should have come to a little stream Cashie had
told him would be there—about so-many paces—it
wasn't there at all, and five hundred paces further
on it still wasn't there. John remembered he'd
begun to walk faster then, so fast that by this time
he should have come across Uncle Cashie's trail—
next he began to run: and came back to that big
windfall he'd scrambled across just a little while
ago—

But Uncle Lon was right, Leonidas Merritt who
knew everything, who was his boss, who was the
crude backwoods tsar of the famous Merritt clan,
who'd sent him and Cashie and Lewis J. up the
Mis-sa-be to look pine-land. "And mind," that
fierce-eyed man had told the three of them, "if you
see any iron-outcrops, or even some bowlders of
drift ore that look like they might amount to something—get that down in your minits, the exact
place of it. And mind you keep your mouths shut
about where you've seen it!" Johnnie smiled: that
was maybe the one thing foolish about Uncle Lon
—this idea of iron on the Mis-sa-be—

Just the same all these days, with their pack-
sacks getting lighter as their grub got lower, lower,
the three of them had each of them kept one eye
cocked at all rocks and chunks of jasper while the
other eye looked up a tree-trunk. Uncle Lon would
be sure to ask them. "And when Uncle Lon got mad

—God!" John E. remembered, long after, with a smile making wrinkles around his mild, kind, gray eyes. "Uncle Lon 'd get over it pretty quick, but while he was coolin' off you damn well wanted to stand out from under!"

Well—Johnnie had done what Leonidas had told him to; in the bowl of his pipe were mostly ashes, and the punky poplar trunks were burned through. The shadows began to come back out of the trees, to sneak back toward him; it was really dark now, and snowing—fit for a blizzard in the open places. He was immensely alone. Cashie and Lewis J.— they were snugged up in camp by now boiling the kettle, it couldn't be far away, since he'd only left them in the middle of the morning. No—he wasn't really lost, and he knocked the dead ashes from his pipe. But a feller can run mighty far from any camp when he's really scared. "And maybe I *wasn't* scared!" thought John E. The fire burned lower. A parade of the ghosts of good cruisers who had run away from camp in these north woods, and never come back at all, began to march through John Merritt's head. He got up, just a wee bit fidgety once more—must make camp, must make camp.

What was that? "Hey-e-e-e—ee!" sounded, very faintly, through the bush. That was Cashie, all right.

"Then—I was mighty ashamed of it," said John

61

E., a little while ago, as he thought back to that momentous day on which Cassius Merritt ran onto his first Mis-sa-be iron, "but those fellers just hollered me back into camp."

"At first I started tryin' to go toward those voices without hollerin' back—so it'd look as if I'd walk in on 'em just natural like. But those confounded yells seemed to come from all over, and I began runnin' again, in the dark too, and hurtin' myself, and God knows what might have happened. But at last I hollered back! . . . Well"—and old John E. Merritt smiled a little shamefacedly, forty years after, at the memory of it—"pretty soon there I was, snugged up for the night, safe in camp, drinking my coffee and eating the pork and doughgod. Maybe that wasn't all right! And maybe you don't think Uncle Cashie and Lewis J. didn't give me an awful joshing!

"They'd *hollered* me into camp!"

II

"IT don't feel so very awful heavy, Cashie, I can't say," and young John Merritt hefted a hunk of rock that Cassius tossed to him. The boy who'd come so very near not coming back to camp the evening before stood now with wrinkled brow, scanning a piece of stone with that appearance of critical sagacity common to all young prospectors who are still very low down in their a-b-c's of prospecting. Here was something—maybe tremendous —that Uncle Cashie had run onto yesterday during those terrible hours while he himself had been lost. John peered with his mild, un-Merritt-like gray eyes at this extremely ancient chunk of America; intent upon what this nondescript bit of the Mis-sa-be hills might mean—he had forgotten yesterday. He was feeling fit as only his rough breakfast, a pipe of tobacco afterwards, and that strangely bracing northern air can make your woods-cruiser feel. Twelve hours of sleep—dreamless—had blotted last evening's horrid fear from his thoughts. He only remembered how Cassius had made an end to that rude joshing about danger so common among men who pass their lives in danger:

"Now, Johnnie, forget it! That might happen to the best of 'em. Only mind you don't make such a darn fool of yourself again. But listen, boy, I saw something today. Lookin' that piece of pine up the slope toward the north, I came across a big rock—looks like iron! Don' know . . . But what say we stroll over tomorrow mornin' and have a look—and maybe take some samples back to Uncle Lon?"

The stroll proved to be a breath-taking, face-scratching, leg-wearying crash through what's commonly called impenetrable forest. But for Cassius Merritt—who in certain highly specialized pursuits was the most extraordinary of the Merritt men— the walk was nothing at all, and like some super-beagle of a sniffing hunter the broad-shouldered younger brother of Leonidas led his slender nephew to the rock of yesterday, knocked a piece off it, handed the boy a hunk of it.

Here they stood, miles from nowhere, as crude, as completely inexpert a pair of mineral experts as you'd find in the whole desolate tangle of the north. They were just a pair of voyageurs looking—and not knowing. A geologist could have told these two gropers in a jiffy that what was exciting them was merely a mound of ferruginous chert, amphibolitic, that what they held in their hands was silica, with

Route of Alf Merritt's "dog trains" toward first great Iron discovery on the Missabe Range

VERMILLION RANGE

Lake Vermillion

Tower

Where first merchantable Ore on the Missabe was struck by the Merritts

Big Rice Lake

Missabe Station

Embarrass Lake

RANGE

Where John E. Merritt was lost in the woods in '84

Mtn. Iron

MISSABE

St. Louis River

Duluth & Iron Range R. R.

To Grand Rapids

Duluth Missabe & Northern R. R.

Route to the Missabe Woods

Vermillion Trail (built by Stunts in the late sixties)

Where Wilbur carried Cashie across the featherbed swamp

Whiteface River

Canoe

St. Louis River

Cloquet River

Two Harbors

Duluth

LAKE SUPERIOR

Oneota

Superior

The MISSABE DISTRICT and the Country explored by the MERRITTS in their Search for Iron

Drawn by R.L. Lambdin

bands and shots of iron oxide—intermediate between hematite and limonite . . . But of course
there was no geologist there; there'd never been one
at this particular spot on the jungle-covered south
slope of the Mis-sa-be hills—miles and miles, and
no trail, west of the good safe canoe-water of the
Embarrass River. Indeed it is doubtful if even
Ojibway Indians had ever been just here.

John E. and his Uncle Cashie had possibly
never heard of ferruginous chert; it was the one
doubtful merit of these entirely unmineralogical
Merritt boys to have got to this certain spot on
Mis-sa-be Wasju.

It was grotesque: here they were, the first men
of all men—maybe—who'd ever seen this rock that
is said by rock-readers to have had such an amazing, checkered history. Compared to the hoary age
of this stone, all the years of their own lives were
less than the wink of an eyelash. Shadowed by
giant white pines now, that rock ten thousand years
before hadn't known what a pine tree looked like,
and thousands of years before that it had perhaps
been completely hidden, oppressed by the giant burden of the continental ice-cap.* Cassius Merritt,
with a sharp eye for nature, with the Merritt imagination too, didn't dream of it, and John E. was of
course then too callow: but this rock over which

* See Appendix C, page 220.

65

they now stood muttering had been old in days
when the earth knew no ice at all. In successive
epochs it had been hidden under salt water that a
man—if there had then been men—could have
cruised clean around the world on. Again, during
unimaginable successions of centuries it had been
good dry land. Then with the rest of the face of
the northern land it had strangely subsided, and
the goggle-eyed, unknown ancestors of our modern
shad and bluefish had—maybe—glided by it again.

The fiercely concentrated, earnest, religious Cassius never thought for a moment of the meaning-
less, idiotic chance that had brought him here for
these few minutes, face to face with a mound of
ironstone that had been born, had settled and sedi-
mented out of water in a remote aeon of time which
has left no sign or record of life at all. But surely
there had been life even then? For in those remote
days unseen, cunning workers had laid this iron
down for the particular benefit, comfort, and use of
men—for humankind whose existence had maybe
not begun for millions of years thereafter.

"Better chuck some hunks of it into your pack-
sack, boy, and take it to Uncle Lon—he'll want it
analyzed," muttered Cassius.

The words, the feelings of John E., were entirely
unromantic as he picked up this product of the toil
of vastly ancient microbes who had worked here by

the Mis-sa-be in days when the earth was not yet inhabited—maybe—by creatures as dignified and highly developed as oysters or clams. Strange, thread-like beings, some shaped like microscopic ribbons, others looking like nothing more than bits of five-thousandths-of-an-inch-long twisted strands of rope, had mayhap in those old days drunk, for the support of their lives, certain salts of iron washed from the backbone of the American Continent. In delicate sheaths around their sub-visible bodies, the iron had gathered, great clots and knots and reddish-brown masses of it. Then they'd died, in their coats of iron. And for stretches of time too fantastically long to divide into years or even millenniums, billions of bodies of these iron-shrouded microbes had settled, drifted, dropped to the bottom, and mixed with sand, and had begun to become cemented there—to be replaced above by succeeding billions of their descendants, energetic silly little beings who worked at this entirely useless job of drinking carbonate of iron and encasing themselves in oxide of iron, in red-iron ore. Useless— until this moment in the year of grace, 1884, when Cassius Merritt, woodsman, had happened by here.

Skin-poor, with their pack-sacks light and their bellies lean, Cassius and his brother Lewis, together with their newly-educated nephew, John E., laced their shoe-packs for the eighty-mile hike back to

Duluth, to report to the powerful Leonidas. Johnnie's pack was a bit heavier than the rest, and contained rocks, legacies of those remote little beings, who, though insignificant, were yet at one time living—and should properly be considered the first heroes of this story and the indispensable forerunners of the Merritt men.

III

OLD Lewis Merritt, the father, had died, down on his farm in Missouri, where he'd justifiably migrated to get out of the damp and the cold—but his own theory, or visionary notion if you will, had survived in the head of Leonidas. Hepzibeth, wife of Lewis and mother of the Merritts, had come back to the Head of the Lakes to live with those of her boys who had always stuck with Duluth. In those days of the middle eighties, at last, they were coming up in the world. Hepzibeth's dark eyes, her straight-lipped mouth, her face with hardly yet a wrinkle, all these were serene at the thought of her sons. Indeed who could be prouder than this little matriarch, for what would Duluth have done without their temperance, their square-shooting honesty, their toughness, and their amazing optimism?

Jerome, the eldest, had been the first school-teacher there, and though he now had died, he'd left stout boys—among them Wilbur the woods-cruiser and the lithe, lean-jawed young Bert. Lucien was a Methodist preacher—and what a preacher! He carried on his father Lewis's stern and uncompromising nonconformity; he was a huge man with a formidable iron-gray beard, a ministerial frock coat and a derby hat settled firmly on the back of his head. His portrait remains; he sits cross-legged with defiant face, with one hand under his vest, fingers hooked behind a suspender: his very appearance would put the fear of God into any backwoods sinner. Yet, it is told how he took into his home a betrayed homeless girl, how his good wife nursed her till her child had come. Hepzibeth smiled with a certain grim tenderness when she thought of Lucien's son, young John E. Merritt—Leonidas was saying Johnnie was getting to be a mighty likely land-looker, explorer.

Maybe Napoleon and Lewis J. would never set the world on fire, but they didn't drink, and some way made ends meet. But look at Alfred. He wore a wide black hat and slouchy clothes; mighty few words came through his walrus mustaches, but what he did mutter was pat, was sensible, was to the point and shrewd. As business men went, in this land still too young to attract the barons of big business, Alfred, her son, was a formidable trader, and remarkable for liking the trials of the bush better than the luxuries that inevitably come with money. About Cassius, Hepzibeth sometimes worried. He was nervous, sweet-tempered, yes, yet given to strange worrying moods. But it was the boast of the Merritt clan that Cashie could pack the whole twelve miles through the woods across a section, throw down his sack, say: "Well—the corner-post ought to be just about here." And he'd hardly be more than twenty feet out of the way.

Hepzibeth smiled her economical smile: Lon, the fourth one—there was the leader! Simply to watch the incredible doings, eloquent prophecies, the dizzily multiplying activities of this son with her husband Lewis's fierce eyes—that was enough to make her content to sit knitting his cruiser's socks for him. It was fun to watch Leonidas, always climbing, reaching, never looking behind him; never mind the four months with snow banked nearly high enough to keep half the daylight out of the windows, and never mind the rainy, half-wintry summers. Her boy Lon was a builder.

. . . . . .

Alas, this stone that his brothers Cassius and Lewis, and his nephew Johnnie, had brought back to Lon from the Mis-sa-be now, was not so much. Johnnie dumped the dusty, multi-colored pieces of rock out of his pack-sack onto the table of Lon's little office, and the thick-necked leader of the Merritts bent his head over it studiously—but hardly knew more about it than his brothers or his decidedly not geological young nephew. And again alas,

71

the report came back from the assayer: "Lean magnetic iron-ore; not merchantable."

This bad news seemed to bother Leonidas not one bit. With a minute exactness that could come only from his own vast knowledge of that wild country, Lon questioned Cassius. They were a strange pair as they stood in that dim little office: Lon knew that Cashie—though the country was totally unsurveyed and far away from water—could take him back like some homing pigeon to the precise spot this iron had come from; Cashie, prince of explorers, blindly following Lon in his grandest schemes. They were a queer contrast, and yet alike, these two brothers Merritt. Lon's sharp eyes glared into the gentler ones of his younger brother. Cassius was much less excitable, less boilingly energetic—and yet a nervousness worked and simmered underneath in him. Both brothers were stamped with the style and trademark of Merritt by their heads, their jaws.

"That's right—you found this iron-outcrop on the *south* slope of the Mis-sa-be, Cashie?"

Cassius brought out his minits, his rough field map, to show Lon the exact spot of it.

"You've never seen anything that looked any good *north* of the crest—the other side of the height of land, have you?"

Cassius shook his head.

"No—I thought no. That's what father always

72

said: The iron, when found, will lie under the brow toward the south."

Lon's was a cocksure science, the very opposite of impartial, open-minded searching. It didn't bother him at all that what old Lewis Howell Merritt had seen—way back in '65—lay far away, better than twenty-five miles away toward the east of the spot where Cashie had just seen this ore. Nor was it a matter of concern to this peculiarly optimistic man that what his father had seen was also poor iron, not merchantable, not a whit better than this that Johnnie had just now brought home. As Leonidas testified, long after, to a solemn committee of Congressmen of the United States of America—on what was probably the third most dramatic day of his life:

"It was a matter of conscience with me. . . . I believed it (the iron) was there because my father was a very intelligent man, and a man that did not go off the handle, and he had studied that up, and I believed it because he told me so, first."

In addition to this virtue of nursing matters of conscience so fiercely, so persistently, Lon was besides a sort of second George R. Stuntz in his ability to bull his way into the woods far away from water, and he was superior to Stuntz in that he had no dreamy, generalized, scientific interests to make him woolgather. He was after white pine and iron,

73

always white pine and iron. Though he was hardly
more than five-feet-eight, he weighed better than a
hundred and eighty, with next to none of it fat,
and in his later years it was his proud memory:

"D'ye know, that although the timber man was
always looking up—and I am a short man—I could
do better than the tall man because the overgrowth
bothered me less, and because of my short legs there
was less leverage for the undergrowth!"

At the Head of the Lakes it became legendary
about him that he scorned the tumpline—that's the
head strap, or, more accurately, the misery strap
which ordinary men used to ease the hundred-
pound load from bearing too full on their shoulders
and backs. Lon Merritt's back and shoulders were
strong enough—plenty. In fact, no villainy of nature nor any purely physical burden ever seemed to
bother him; against trees, windfalls, underbrush,
black-flies and wolves he was always triumphant.
Leonidas would maybe always have had plain sail-
ing, gotten enormously rich, had no heartache or
tragedy, if it weren't that he was always viewing
people as objects for battles, conflicts. He would
have come through all right, if it hadn't been that,
when it came to sarcastic vituperation, Lon had the
gift of tongues. . . . And yet the whole north
country knew he would give anybody the shirt off
his back.

IV

A WISE man has worked it out, and proved, I believe, that time is the fourth dimension of everything; of this discovery your present story-teller understands neither the mathematics nor the philosophy. But surely, to produce the present clanging, hammering, high-reaching, proud and comfortable age of steel, *successions of events* have been of enormous importance. It is fantastic to remember how the immense rocky northern platform, that backbone of the American Continent on which Lon and his band were now playing out their proud and pitiful little drama, should have been born in fire so many aeons ago—bringing iron up into the boiling waters. Then, before there were any intelligent creatures at all to feel the lack of iron ore, came primitive life, came immensely ancient microbes to prepare it. Surely there's a kindly God, who created those absurd little *Gallionella*—though nobody knows now what He called the iron-eating microbes—but anyway here were these sub-visible beings, planted there to toil for numberless millenniums laying down the iron, convenient in basins, lenses—

This iron, it's almost certain, was afterward covered by sediments, which congealed into enormous masses of rock, so thick a hundred Lon Merritts could never have sniffed the iron out from under them. But no matter: convenient myriads of centuries passed—before there were men—so that wind, so that water, could wear these protecting rocks away, and enrich the deposits of iron. Yet it was maybe still not exposed, or ready to use, when fishes and oysters were the proud owners of America, nor when successions of lizards, dinosaurs, mastodons, and saber-toothed tigers, had their geologic day in dominating what's now for a moment *our* country. But what did that matter, because what would those slimy, ferocious, and unenlightened creatures have done with iron, anyway?

Then for a long time, and maybe several times,* the crunching white masses and the vast cold doom of the continental ice-cap hid Lake Superior's rim, but it was of absolutely no consequence: if there were men to the south—*if* there were—they were slant-browed savages with no notion of how iron might be forged into suspension bridges, motor cars, plows, bathrooms, and baby buggies. But how marvelous was this glacier, and how wise the Great Hand that melted it, for while this epic thaw almost uncovered a strange tremendous deposit of iron,

* See Appendix C, page 220.

it left blue water that would be the one proper, cheap, convenient way to carry that iron to men who would later need it. From this melt, so perfectly timed in our succession of events, it was only a geological hour till hybrid millions of men, modern, clever—call them *Homo sapiens* if you will—swarmed over the Alleghenies and on to the prairies; and they were full of a tilling and building energy generated—maybe—by this very fact of their first generation hybridity. They stretched out their hands, called for iron, wanted inexhaustible millions of tons of red ore to smelt into pig iron to convert into steel. They were ably led, and their leaders—capitalists, iron-masters—bawled and roared for ore that must be cheaper, cheaper, to cut the costs in the newly-begun standardized production of—everything.

Now we come, suddenly, out of the murky ruck of ancient time, to the middle eighties of the nineteenth century. At this point in the long and logical march of happenings, there is a tiny occurrence, a seemingly insignificant concatenation of events at the Head of the Lakes. In its own way it is as lucky, as happy for all of us, as necessary for America's arrogant age of steel, as any of the more remote, more grandiose, more spectacular acts of God. The damp north country around Lake Superior's rim is aswarm with iron hunters now. Pros-

pectors, geologists, professors of the science of minerals, practical mining men—are drilling, theoriz-
ing, exploring, test-pitting, for the ore that's now
being sucked down the lakes into Carnegie's blast
furnaces; into a hundred other flaring, roaring mid-
western stoves the ore goes in an endless stream of
long lean boats. But where's cheaper ore, endlessly
abundant iron to be had for a song? In the scientific reports of that day, not a geologist would have
risked his name to say there was more ore, cheaper
ore, than that already found on the Marquette, the
Menominee, the Gogebic, and the Vermilion Iron
Ranges.

But at this very moment there exist Leonidas
Merritt and his band of brothers. Leonidas is absolutely uneducated, in the formal and accepted
sense, in the science of rock-reading; what is worse,
in the few of his writings that remain, now yellowed
by time—for these were the defiant writings of his
heyday in the nineties—you will find all experts
lumped together under the scornful designation of
"scientific squirts!" Not only must such sarcastic
disrespect be held as a black mark against Leonidas, but he might, in those early days, have been
very properly denounced as a fool and a visionary
for not sticking to his timber cruising.

Professor Chester had come, and George Stuntz
—who certainly could command even the contemp-

tuous Leonidas's respect—had shown Chester real
iron mines by Vermilion Lake. But, having been
chaperoned by Stuntz pretty thoroughly over the
eastern end of the Mis-sa-be Heights, the Professor had very properly condemned this desolate region. Lon himself would have had to admit the
professor's accuracy; for to this day no respectable
iron deposit has been uncovered on the Mis-sa-be
east of the Embarrass River—which was where
Stuntz and Chester went. The brilliant geological
family of the Winchells, of whom the head was the
sagacious old Alexander, had ranged these hills,
had made close studies of its rocks, had found never
an ounce of iron fit to sell or to smelt. The noted
rock-reader, Irving, had cruised as far away from
water as you'd expect a geologist to do; he'd
dubbed the iron-bearing Mis-sa-be rocks "Animikie," discovered a lot about their enormous age, and
found no hint of real iron. Yet our bull-headed chief
of what he liked to call the Ne-con-dis—the band of
brothers—came near breaking the backs of his
brothers, Alfred, Cassius, and his nephews, John E.
and Wilbur, sending them back, and back up there.
His was an unheard-of, an extravagant, an idiotic
persistence.

Even if he was so intensely parochial, so narrow-
minded as to turn up his nose at geologists, scientists, Lon might have taken a hint from the failures

of men of his own craft, bushwhackers, landlookers.
Peter Mitchell of Ontonagon had made diggings
and they'd come to no good. When the Duluth and
Iron Range Railroad was cut across the Mis-sa-be
to Stuntz's mines on Lake Vermilion, the cruisers
Mallman and Geggie had seen suspicious red
streaks, that were said by the historian Van Brunt
"to have shouted iron." But they followed these
streaks—and came back to Duluth with empty
pack-sacks. Gil Goff, looking land west from
Grand Rapids for the Saginaw pine-dukes, did report: "In '83 I done land-looking—and seen iron,"
but his alleged observations came to nothing. Even
the able David Adams came back from the western
Mis-sa-be in the middle eighties with empty hands.
To the complete hopelessness of all these ventures
the official Monograph No. 43 of the United States
Geological Survey testifies:

"Since the late sixties . . . not a single deposit
of iron ore of such size and character as to warrant
exploration had been shown up. In fact the range
had been turned down by many mining men who
examined it."

Yet Leonidas strained his own back, and his
bank-book too, plodding back up in there, again,
again.

Established iron companies, like the Minnesota
Iron Company, not headed by visionaries, but by

HEPZIBETH WITH LEONIDAS AT HER LEFT; JOHN E., SEATED, AT EXTREME LEFT; REV. LUCIEN, SEATED, AT EXTREME RIGHT, 1889

"YET LEONIDAS STRAINED HIS OWN BACK, AND HIS BANK, TOO, PLODDING BACK UP IN THERE, AGAIN, AGAIN." LEONIDAS, JOHN E., AND BERT, ON PORTAGE, 1889

men like Charlemagne Tower, sent the best men they could hire to Mis-sa-be. The geologist H. V. Winchell wrote of these wild-goose chases: "Iron experts of good repute were sent to examine the outcrops of ore known at that time . . . The journey was an arduous one into a dense wilderness, and there is no wonder they did no test-pitting or drilling. They were sent to examine outcrops, which they properly enough condemned, for the only iron to be seen was in thin strata of magnetite banded with jaspery quartz."

Lon Merritt kept following his conscience.

V

"OH, Wilbur—hold up a minute," called Cassius Merritt, "my knee's on the bum—can't go no further."

The two of them were in the unsurveyed, trackless bush, ten days out from Duluth on the soggy upland, beyond the Cloquet and the Whiteface River—half-way toward the Mis-sa-be Heights. Wilbur, son of the dead eldest of the Merritt brothers, Jerome, was much younger than Cassius. He stopped, put up his compass, remembered not to forget the exact number of paces he'd made west, after turning from north. Wilbur was worried, and who blames him? For three days out of Duluth with their sacks still heavy with grub, their shoe-pacs had stubbed against the stones, tripped over roots, sunk into the sodden bogs of the Vermilion Trail. Then they'd struck off into the bush; for seven days they'd run absolutely by their compasses, laboriously, monotonously counting every last single pace, so many thousands to the west, another couple of thousand to the south, so many west again—

84

Every day of these seven days black-flies had jabbed them, bled them, feasted merrily off them. Mosquitoes, gray hordes of them, had bitten even the palms of their hands in the evenings as they crouched over their campfires—dead beat—cooking their beans and sow-belly; those insects had hummed exasperating lullabies, and occasionally sneaked in through holes in the gauze of their fly-tight tent at dawn. Seven days, and no pine, no pine worth mentioning in their minits, and now Cassius, whom nothing could hurt—

Wilbur looked at his uncle, watched the weathered tan of his face turn a sallow yellow with pain, saw him throw off his pack-sack, sink to the ground. Oh, well—in the morning; and Wilbur made camp, boiled the kettle, and slept his cruiser's sleep on his balsam boughs. In the morning Cashie's knee was worse; in fact, it was no good whatever. He growled with the pain of it and cursed his confounded leg as it suddenly went limp on him as he tried to stand. Wilbur looked at Cassius, all of one hundred and eighty pounds of bone and muscle; what were you going to do with a one-legged man in the bush fifty miles from home, with less than ten days' grub, and no grub between you and Duluth? Cassius said nothing; he looked pitifully absurd as strong men sometimes do when they're out of kilter; he tried to move, only growled. Wilbur got busy with his ax,

and here—presto—was a trough made from a hol-
low tree trunk; he set the camp kettles to boiling
over a great blaze of fire; he heated stones, and kept
water hot in the trough by dropping those stones
into it; he soaked extra pairs of socks in the trough,
wrung them out, wrapped them round Cashie's
knee. "We'll get the pain out of it," said Wilbur.

Next morning the pain was worse; and of grub
there was one day less; and they hadn't moved.

"You'd better leave me here, kid, and pace your
way out to the Vermilion Trail, mark where you
hit it, hike to Duluth, and bring back Alf and Lon
and the boys," said Cassius.

"I'd thought of that," said Wilbur. He didn't
tell Cashie of other things he'd thought of, getting
lost, getting held up himself, coming back many
days later, miscounting his paces, missing Cashie's
lonely camp—or, worse still, getting back with help
and finding Cassius gone, perhaps driven into the
jungle by a delirium of pain, or by that fatal confusion of judgment that gets your best man when
he's alone and helpless in the woods. "I'd thought
of that—but no, guess we better stick together."

Wilbur's busy again, cutting saplings. "Here,
old boy—try these," he calls to Cassius. He helps
him up, and under his arms he puts a pair of saplings, cut down just the right distance from their
crotches, for crutches. Camp is broken, the last dish

washed and stowed, the precious grub packed away
in its unbleached cotton bags, and there they go
through the bush, as strange a little procession as
any you've seen. Wilbur, barge of a man that he
is, bends under the weight of both their pack-sacks,
and runs the compass—Cassius, no longer a leader,
hobbles behind on his absurd pair of crutches. They
come to an open place, it looks light—and cheerful.
"We ought to make the Whiteface River by tomorrow noon," says Wilbur. "Then I'll build you
a raft that'll knock your eye out, and we'll float
right down into the St. Louis, and to Fond du
Lac—"

Cassius looks at the country ahead. "You see
what we're in for, Wilbur. Just try your foot on
that ground!"

Wilbur tries; it's a nice level-looking stretch of
country, almost treeless except for here and there a
clump of tamarack, and dwarf spruce and balsam
fir grouped in graceful spires. The ground is hum-
mocky, but lovely with little bushes that look as if
they might have blueberries on them. Wilbur puts
his weight on his feet—and sinks in nearly to his
knee. "Better leave me here—I'll never get across
this mess," says Cassius.

"You wait here for a bit, Cashie." And the tall,
lean-faced, heavy-jawed youngster is off, with both
pack-sacks, across that sinister featherbed swamp

that sucks him downward at every step, till his groin is sore, till his mouth tastes—coppery. Now he's back, having left the duffle a quarter of a mile ahead.

"You see, Uncle, you're in luck; you're goin' to have a ride across this here damn swamp."

Pick-a-back he carries the one hundred and eighty pounds of helpless Cassius Merritt.

All day so: pack-sacks first, then the marvelous, light-shouldered, restful walk back to Cassius with no load at all, then the stumbling, dreadful trek, every step as far downward, and upward, out of the soggy moss—*farther* downward and upward than it carries them ahead. That night they sleep somehow in the middle of the morass, on a platform Wilbur cuts from dried spruce saplings, with their tent pitched anyhow over it. By next noon—hurrah— the ground gets higher; Cassius can navigate on his crutches again; by night they've reached the blessed Whiteface River.

Two days, and they're floating down the innocent, smooth-looking surface of it, on a rotten raft, a raft made from poplar that would water-log in less than no time, but poplar was all Wilbur had.

"Put all the grub in one sack, boy, and mind you lash it to your bum home-made boat," says Cashie with a grin, which, by practice, he has developed to hide his pain. "You don't know this river like I do. Those rapids—"

This is the life of Reilly for them. It's great for Cassius not to feel those saplings under his chafed armpits; and for Wilbur there are no packs to carry, no compass to run, no paces to count. The raft goes faster; they run a couple of riffles—swift, though hardly yet white water—that Wilbur guides his loggy ship through with expert, canoeman's jabs of his spruce setting-pole. The raft goes still faster, altogether too fast now. "You'd better land her," yells Cassius—and from around the bend, very close, there's a menacing, continuous roar. But the raft is no birch-bark boat; Wilbur sweats, gives the ultimate ounce of himself to his pole. The roar is deafening now, and it hides the crash as the poor little craft goes to pieces as it sucks over the brink into the boil of the rapids.

Two of the strongest of the house of Merritt disappear in a booming swirl of waves and foam—and one of them is totally, almost totally helpless. . . .

"Hey—Wilbur! Here I am!" yells Cassius.

Some way, heaven knows how, Cassius had held onto a log of poplar, had got swept into an eddy, had even recovered their pack-sack as it bobbed about, lashed to a timber. Some way Wilbur, caught in the dreadful rush and tearing power of the worst of the white water, had been bruised and bumped against rocks, but not sucked under. For the eddy he had struck out, wild with worry for the crippled Cassius. "Why, Cashie! you're walkin'! What the devil!"

"I *had* to use that knee, gettin' away from those rocks and into the eddy, boy—an' now she's all right, she's fine!"

Cassius looked at the giant Wilbur, who was making faces while he rubbed his banged-up knees and elbows, who looked bedraggled and ridiculous, who presently laughed a lumberjack's bellow of a laugh. He was alive! Cassius laughed too: "I want no more of your rotten rafts, boy—nor your home-made crutches. Here's a great place to camp—an' tomorrow we'll be walkin' home!"

"You might have got your knee back in kilter before I started totin' you across that —— feather-bed swamp," groused Wilbur, and he qualified the morass with epic northern adjectives, not fit for print.

"But, boy—now I know what a man you are. Wasn't goin' to fix my knee till I found out how good you were. Boy—you are one real packer!" And Wilbur was; and having it told him, even in a josh, was meat and drink to him. They made their camp; they dried their tobacco—first. And before the fire this night Cassius and Wilbur Merritt,

90

three hours beyond what should have been death, tasted that peculiar salt of life: the glow that comes with looking back on your bitter day's work and liking the very bitterness of it. Next day they kidded each other back toward Duluth—no matter no pine, they were alive. Such were the younger Merritts. So they learned every part of that blank dreary land that stretched from Duluth to the Missa-be hills. Such were the men the leaders, Leonidas and Alfred, knew they could bank on.

VI

In the high summer of what was probably '88, though the exact year is in dispute, Cassius Merritt found real iron, excellent hematite, merchantable ore on the Mis-sa-be Heights. He ran across a chunk of it in Section 31 of Town 58 North, Range 18 West of the Fourth Principal Meridian of Minnesota. He wasn't on a cruise looking for iron—excepting that, obedient to Leonidas, he forever had an eye open for it; his job just now was that of head explorer for a corps of engineers. He was showing these engineers where to locate their road, because they were making a preliminary survey for what they hoped was going to be a railroad from Duluth all the way northwest to Winnipeg. It turned out to be an imaginary railroad, an air-castle of a line that has never come to exist in reality to this day. But for this story that doesn't matter at all. What matters is that just at the geographical Height of Land on the Central Mis-sa-be, Cassius Merritt picked up a heavy hunk of pure iron. It was at that significant, mysterious spot where all the little springs to the north of him headed for bleak Hudson Bay, where all the creeks to the south of him did their bit to help fill the Gulf of Mexico and the Atlantic Ocean. Cassius had come to this spot simply and purely because this was the easiest grade over the Mis-sa-be on the line from Duluth to Winnipeg.

He put the chunk of iron in his pack-sack and shut his mouth about it. He expertly led the survey of experts all the way to the wild country at the crossing of the Big Fork River; from there on Cashie completed a topographical survey all the way north to the Canadian line, to the nine-mile-post, west of the Lake of the Woods. On September 3d he got back to Duluth; honestly he told of his iron find to his boss, Mr. Rogers, who with M. B. Harrison was duly impressed by it. He then went to Leonidas—with permission—and said:

"Lon, you're right. There's real iron on the Mis-sa-be."

—Though all Cassius had seen was one bowlder of it, and not at all a mine or any extensive outcrops. But this was enough for Leonidas Merritt. The place where Cashie had found it was, with his entirely characteristic accuracy, marked down to the dot. It was, so Lon pointed out triumphantly, only two looks and a holler from the other place, where Cassius had spotted that great mound of lean ore, on the day, three years before, when young

John E. had got himself so foolishly lost. In their long, visionary, hide-and-go-seek game for iron, there is no doubt that Lon and Alf were now getting warm, getting hot.

It was a great piece of luck for the Merritts that they were just now on the up; their fifteen fly-bitten, break-boned years of pine-looking were at last bringing cash, real money. "Why, we were that flush we could actually hire a packer, to tote our grub in for us," said John E., long after. And when they ran out of money, Lon and Alf would sell off another rich pine location, and soak the cash that came from it into new exploring parties. In '89, the year after Cassius had found that fine chunk of pure ore, the Merritts literally swarmed over the Mis-sa-be hills; Leonidas, Cassius, the stolid, shrewd Alfred, Wilbur, and his lean-jawed young brother Bert, Lewis J. and John E.—whom by now you couldn't lose anywhere—began a gigantic and foolish search of Lon's devising. I say foolish, because almost all of the wise heads, the old-timers of the head of the lakes, thought it was not only foolish, but downright crazy—

Why try what not only scientific geniuses, but practical, sensible prospectors had given up long ago? Everybody knew the only place there was iron in the whole north country was up toward Lake Vermilion. Now it's perfectly true that Leonidas had sent off John E. and Cassius to that water-infested country, to make their first magnetic surveys—and this shakes somewhat the legend that Lon had primary faith in the profitless Mis-sa-be hills from the start. But Lon's luck was with him; in a way he was *forced* southwest toward the Mis-sa-be Heights—because the rich and powerful Minnesota Iron Company had picked up nearly all of the "good stuff"—as Lon called it—round Lake Vermilion. These wealthy, successful operators wanted no part of Mis-sa-be, had been told it was worthless, by mine captains and professors. So here are Lon and his crew, plodding back and forth through the woods of the Grandmother Hills, willy-nilly. From this it must not be understood that Lon hadn't followed his conscience, hadn't kept faith in his father's strange prophecy. But it's well to remember that events, and human motives leading up to triumphs, to tragedies, are not simple, but are, on the other hand, full of chances, improvisations, whimsies of fate, complexities.

"Well, let 'em have the Vermilion, then," Leonidas may well have stormed, in a council of the Merritt brothers. He was perfectly ready to resume their searching anywhere else, with the faith that somewhere they'd find—something. Such was his gusto, his incredible exuberance, and these were a thousand times more important than his knowledge

Burns Camp. Aug. 21. 1887
We have carefully run over the
9 Lots indicated on annexed map
and find from 30 to 90 degrees.
dip on all lands enclosed in
the line marked thus x x x x
I have indicated the outcrops of
Jasper & Iron that we saw
by sed shade thus ::::::::::
We got 25° dip outside of
Line marked by cross but
nothing less than 25 inside.

You will see that the widest
body of attraction is on the
quarter Line of Sec.

There is a test Drift just
east of Lot one on Lake Shore &
60° dip there
We found lots of Black Jasper drift
on north Line of Lot 3 but only 20°
dip. a party are sinking test-pits 20
rods west of ¼ post on west side of.
Sec. 30 – 63 – 11.

(Reported by. C.C. & J.E. Merritt.)
to Lon Merritt.

"MINITS" OF 1887 EXPLORATIONS OF CASSIUS AND
JOHN E. MERRITT

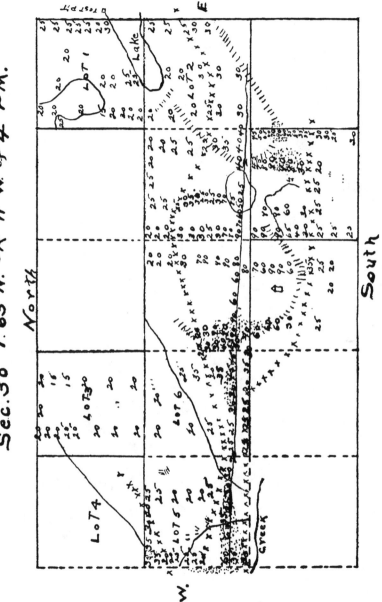

FACSIMILE OF FIELD MAP OF MAGNETIC SURVEY OF VERMILION RANGE BY CASSIUS AND JOHN E. MERRITT
Later developed into the famous "Section 30" mine.

of where iron might or might not be. He insisted on a survey, to be made with a dip-needle compass, on a grand scale along the whole Mis-sa-be Range, from Embarrass Lake to the Mississippi. On this remarkable research he sent John E. and Cashie,* and John E. was a mighty reliable fellow at running the dip-needle, having learned this by no means simple art from the old Michigan iron-hunter, George Fay, from Marquette. There go John E. and his Uncle Cassius, zig-zagging solemnly back and forth along the shin-tangled southern slope of the Mis-sa-be hills, for miles, and more and more brush-beset miles. Every hundred paces, or sometimes every fifty, or on certain precise, important occasions every twenty-five steps—the earnest-faced, long-wispy-mustached John Merritt stops. He turns, faces exactly, carefully west, holds up his queer brass-rimmed instrument before his peering gray eyes, and waits for the dancing, nervous, vibrating needle to come as near as it can to rest. And every now and again he calls to Cashie, in a monotonous sing-song: "Dip—sixty!" "Dip—fifty!" "Dip—twenty-five!"

Cashie jots down each amount of the needle's deflection on the maps of his minits—made with his own incomparable accuracy. On those maps, rows of high numbers—50's, 60's, 75's—begin to grow

* See Appendix D, page 221.

in curious, irregular, wavy lines. Is it iron ore, real iron ore under their feet, that's calling their finicky, vibrating needle? They see never a hint of iron. They call it a day and go back to camp. There Lon waits for them, and before the fire that evening the three of them, and Alf and Wilbur besides, peer at the lines of numbers that Cassius has scrawled along his map of the Mis-sa-be hillside.

"Look at this!" cries Leonidas, and he takes off the tropical pith helmet he absurdly wears in this bleak northern country. "Damned if it don't look like your line of greatest magnetic attraction follows a kind of shore-line!" The uncouth heads of the five of them come together to follow Lon's finger, as it goes over the map lighted by the uncertain flare of their camp-fire. "See!" says Leonidas, "here's a deep bay—and right along here— you've got a headland—"

What could all this mean? The matter-of-fact Alfred said nothing, tactfully, because he knew of old his brother Lon's strange and riotous imagination. "Now I've a theory," Lon began again, and he proceeded to embroider to his brothers, his nephews, what must have sounded like a lot of fantastic nonsense; he invented a story of how iron may possibly have been laid down, out of water, against this theoretical ancient strand . . . of how it was now covered over—"You know, boys, there's been ice here—that's left clay and gravel . . ."

Alfred smiled a little, discreetly, behind his walrus mustache. Where was the iron? Where was any iron at all excepting that one bowlder Cashie had found last year? Heaven knew Alf had been digging for it these last months—

It's a comical, rather brave, somewhat pitiful picture you see—of this gang of impossible scientists, beards on them, the smell of the sweat of the day's fruitless digging and bushwhacking clinging to them, as they plan and argue before their camp-fire. They sit there in their Mackinaw pants and heavy socks, their cow-hide boots steaming close by. Lon's pipe coal flits about like some bobbing gigantic fire-fly, as he propounds his unacademic, unorthodox home-made science in his own geologic jargon. Here are no savants, with pupils. To Lon's expostulations there is no accompaniment of rustling pages of notebooks of respectful students— but only the crackle of the blazing squaw-wood and birch, and sometimes the sudden crash through the bush of a moose, and the occasional far-off cry of a wolf, and always the croon of the northern night wind in the boughs of the white pines above them.

"Throw on a hunk of wood, Johnnie—time to turn in." They get up, grunt, stretch themselves enormously, go about the camp's bedtime duties—

VII

WHILE John E. and Uncle Cashie were doing their mapping for magnetic attraction—and being laughed at by old-timers down in Duluth, for everybody knew that the magnetic iron in that country was too lean, no good—Alfred had started digging holes in the Mis-sa-be crest above them. In March of '89 this plodding citizen had started into the bush from Tower—the town where in winter a six-foot thermometer with zero at the top was wanted, to tell men how cold it really got. "With six men and three dog trains—toboggans—we went by way of Pike River and across Rice Lake, and we were the dogs," muttered Alfred. Of the Merritt boys, Alf was at this time the only one you might call a practical miner. Back in the early seventies he had, in the intervals between a dozen other more or less profitless activities, cracked rock, and dug underground in a vain hunt for fabled copper on Isle Royale in Lake Superior.

Close by where Cashie had found his hunk of fine ore the year before, they stopped, after days of toil through the snow when on some days eight hours of pulling, pushing, hacking, cursing and grunting had carried them forward three-quarters of a mile, no more. They cut down pines with their cross-cut saws, and built a camp from the fallen trees. Alf at the head of them, working slowly, steadily, and as hard as any, these six men began digging holes on the Mis-sa-be crest—till, after weeks, they struck the banded taconite, with a little iron in it, till, after months, they struck ancient fire-stone, granite with next to no iron at all. "It must be deeper," said Alfred to Lon. And Leonidas, grotesque in his white coat, smoked glasses, and pith helmet, hurried back to Duluth, sold more pine land, bought diamond drills and engines, hired gangs of men and cut a tote road twenty-seven miles west through the woods all the way from Mesaba Station of the D. and I. R. railroad, to get in the drills and the engines to run them.

Alf and his men drilled, through lean-iron taconite, and into the granite, and found no iron. The summer was passing; the sumac and the wild cherry were getting ready to set the country aflare with yellow and red. "There's nothing here, Lon," said Alfred. And for want of something better they agreed to dig, next spring, down the slope farther south. During the winter southward they cut their trails. Spring of 1890 was here now, with its melting snow, to the tune of a harshly musical, ecstati-

OLD LEWIS H. MERRITT'S HOTEL AT OWETA. STANDING, LEFT TO RIGHT: ALFRED, LEONIDAS, LUCIEN, NAPOLEON, JOHN E., ANDRUS, AND LEWIS J.

ALFRED'S DIAMOND DRILLING CAMP, ON MISSABE, BEFORE DISCOVERY OF IRON, 1890

cally hopeful twittering of song-sparrows, and with a low mysterious gurgling of a thousand rills of snow water trickling south beneath the pine needles. Once more Alf, Leonidas, and their men began digging, farther south, always a little farther; and the ground was strangely soft and reddish, and they abandoned their diamond drills. They were past the line where Cashie and Johnnie's compass had shown its maximum dip. Wasn't it here they should have turned up ore? Together they peered over the maps on their minits. Still they found no iron, but only taconite, only worthless, jaspery rock. "Let's try it a bit farther south," agreed Alf and Lon.

Now strange things began to happen: the wheels of their lumber wagons sank through the carpet of pine needles, got bogged in deep ruts, red ruts of a peculiar, powdery red soil—heavy. Alfred picked up handfuls of it, hefted it, handed it to his men, to Lon. "That's iron," he said, and was enormously puzzled, and tugged at his magnificent mustache. "It can't be nothing else than float ore. Don't believe a mine could lay this way—close to the top like this. And it's fine, too fine, like dirt. What we want is a *vein* of ore—" Near by in the bush, too, they saw strange signs, and didn't particularly heed them. Here was a spot where a deer had scuffed up the pine needles, laid bare the ground, red ground and heavy. . . .

103

They ran out of money once more. At their wit's end, both of them returned to Duluth, leaving their test-pit crew in the bush, and tried to raise the cash to go on. "We were then rushing around town to get money to pay these expenses," testified Leonidas, long after, before Congressman Stanley and his solemn Congressional Committee. "We had spent then $20,000 on the Mountain Iron, I remember . . . We had a miner in there, a German, who was a good miner, as miners go, you know. He was a good man, an honest, straightforward man."

This good, honest, and straightforward man was Captain J. A. Nicols, at the head of the Merritt test-pit crew. To Captain Nicols, Lon and Alf had given orders to keep going south, to dig down at the foot of the hill. By these orders the good Captain was offended, and who blames him, for he was a man experienced in the lay of land where you might expect, on the grounds of both theory and practice, to find iron. So the Captain and his men climbed back toward the crest, and started work again—where Alfred had already failed for a hopeful, dismal, year and a half.

It looked as if the money might be raised, from more pine land sold, or mortgaged, and the brothers came, in the middle of November of 1890, back to the clearing on the hillside. They came back to find that the good, honest and straightforward Ger-

104

man had disobeyed their orders; and doom for all straightforward Germans flared in Leonidas Merritt's eyes.

"Here, now, we've worked long enough on this rim, let's go down in the basin and sink a pit," shouted Lon.

Nicols was disgusted, and nobody should blame him, and nobody did blame him, excepting maybe the indomitable Leonidas and the silent but shrewd Alfred. "He said he had some reputation as a mining man, which he had," said Leonidas, "and he did not propose to be called, with the rest of us, farmers. They used to call us farmers and lumberjacks and all that sort of thing, in derision. . . . We told him to come to Duluth, and we would send up men that did not have any reputation as miners!"

Then, while Lon exhorted, Alfred grabbed a shovel, drove it through the pine needles into the soft earth—shovel after shovelful he turned up. . . . Nicols looked, then gaped. While Lon argued, Alf said it—with shovels.

So Leonidas won his discussion. Nicols gave in, and agreed to dig where Lon told him to dig. Alfred and Leonidas went back to Duluth, being, alas, not yet quite sure about getting their money. The next morning—this was the 16th of November of 1890—the honest Nicols started digging again, not quite where Lon had ordered him to nor yet

105

where Alf had shown him real iron, but, being a stubborn as well as a straightforward man, a little way back up the hill. What happened that day is history, and should be recorded solemnly, and without excitement. Let it be transcribed from the Twentieth Annual Report, Minnesota Geological Survey, Part IV, entitled "The Mesabi Iron Range," by Horace V. Winchell, F.G.S.A.:

"On the sixteenth day of November, 1890, workmen under the direction of Capt. J. A. Nicols, of Duluth, Minnesota, encountered soft hematite in a test-pit on the northwest quarter of section three, township fifty-eight, range eighteen, west of the fourth principal meridian. This mine, now called the Mountain Iron, was the first body of soft ore discovered on the Mesabi iron range."

The next day the good Captain Nicols came back to Duluth, to Alfred and Leonidas, with fifty pounds of rich, marvelous, 64 percent iron in his pack-sack. He came back, converted, asking the elated Leonidas and the never-excited Alfred:

"What are we going to do? People have been attracted here and they have already come . . . There are trails here and they are looking this country over. What shall we do, cover this up and leave it?"

It is their day of days. It is the beginning of the vindication of old Lewis Howell Merritt's outlandish prophecy, made twenty-five years before to his rising and lusty young band of buckos, to Leonidas, to Alfred in the log house by the bay in Oneota. It is the real start of the proof of George Stuntz's prediction that here, in this Godforsaken northwest land, is the commercial heart of the continent.

"Cover it up!" says Leonidas, with a snort, to Captain Nicols. "You go on there and dig. We want ore. We want to build a railroad to it. You go on there and dig, and find the bottom of that ore. You open it up."

So the Merritts and their men began to dig, toward wonders they themselves nor their dead father had ever dreamed of. Not a year, not a month were these bushwhackers ahead of their time —for the furnaces down below must have iron ore, limitless millions of tons of red, blue, black and purple ore, for the age of steel, for America the iron-hungry Gargantua. They wouldn't, like George Stuntz, have to be content with eight dollars a day, and a destitute death in the Red Cross Hospital. No rich men had helped them to their discovery: they'd grubstaked themselves. They owned the iron —and what power now didn't lie before them? So they started to dig.

PART THREE

PIU PRESTO

"By eleven o'clock that first night, we were all asleep, and slept like tired healthy men call sleep."

JOHN E. MERRITT

I

IT WAS Leonidas Merritt against the world now; America and the whole world wanted iron; on the Mis-sa-be the Merritt clan had dug it up—and Leonidas, in his characteristic and peculiarly individual way, was sure he could show, sell, give America iron in quantities no furnaceman nor miner ever dreamed of.

Hardly a man in the north country around the Head of the Lakes could stand up to Leonidas in the days of his heyday—so what chance had poor Nicols? Buried under an avalanche of turbulent and unreasonable arguments, Nicols could only dig himself out from under them and go back up to the Mis-sa-be, to dig, as Lon had told him to do.

The honest and straightforward Captain had tried one last objection with the bull-necked head of the Merritt clan, had urged Lon to stop digging for the winter, at least, had attempted to get his uncouth chieftain to hide, to cover up what they'd found. "You see," warned Nicols, "these expert geologists will be attracted, and they'll come up there—"

Somehow the cautious Captain seemed to sense the enormity of the iron treasure that their little test-pit, still only fourteen feet deep, had uncovered. No fool was Nicols, and down in him he felt, maybe, his own and even Lon Merritt's littleness, felt their inadequacy to develop this iron for which captains of industry, and hard-boiled down-lakes furnacemen—for which a whole rapacious, savagely building, iron-hungry young nation was reaching.

"These experts, these geologists—" continued Nicols—

"Geologists—experts!" Lon laughed a bellow of a laugh that told Nicols and anybody else who wanted to hear of it, his contempt for all merely learned men. "I don't care *who* those men are," roared Leonidas, "they will come up there, and they will say it is not ore at all! You go on and uncover all the ore you can. We'll risk it!"

Who were geologists, indeed, to compare with the Merritt boys, the band of brothers and nephews, the close-knit gang of weather-beaten frontiersmen that Lon, with his strong feeling for Indian language and poetry, loved to call "The Ne-con-dis." For twenty years, experts of all kinds, and old-timers too, had been calling the men of the Ne-con-dis harebrained, had called them crazy to believe in the Mis-sa-be Range, had smiled—but now, at last, the Merritts could laugh; and if they,

112

the band of brothers, had actually found this strange, soft, new kind of red and purple heavy ore that had lain hidden—carelessly but so very cunningly—under the pine needles among the roots of the white pines, well? Well—what couldn't the Merritts do? So in his pride asked Leonidas.

And yet, in the face of the big parade of finding, digging, transporting, smelting, building, and using iron—for this is what the America of the early 'nineties essentially was—what did these seven or eight Merritt iron men amount to? True enough, they were a gallant band: Alfred was a combination of superlative lumberjack and shrewd business-man; to Cassius no Minnesota explorer could hold a candle; the slender but wiry John E. was a heroic bushwhacker; that barge of a woodscruiser, Wilbur, could turn his hand to anything; Bert, the lean-jawed son of Jerome, was surely a comer; and to help out at a pinch there were the lesser, but at that time still loyal brothers—Lewis J., and Napoleon. And yet, considering the possible vastness of the treasure up there, Leonidas should have taken thought, should have gone easy, should have played his cards close to his chest, should have been—*prudent,* that's the precise word for it. . . .

Because steel—so says an anonymous philosopher—was right at this moment growing to be the heart of civilization, was touching the lives of everybody, was altogether too big a thing for any one man, or seven men, or even a thousand men to pick up, casually. The wise iron-hunter and iron-poet, Chase Salmon Osborn, has told of the vast mystical pageant of iron that America at this time was growing to be. And, in view of the hugeness, the impersonal power of that parade, if Leonidas—and the rest of the Merritt tribe who were cutting, blasting, digging away there in the woods of Mis-sa-be —could only have realized, could only have followed, with Osborn's imagination, their new iron ore into its destinations, its manifold uses—

For Osborn recites how these were the years when America—by means of iron—was just getting into her stride in the gigantic job of turning the dark soil of the whole Mid-West into corn to feed herself, into grain to feed the world. That black earth would have meant nothing without steel plowshares to turn it, steel drills to seed it, strong iron harvesters to reap its produce, mills with rolls of the finest steel to mash and grind its hard grain into flour. If only Leonidas Merritt had really sensed this America with its better than ten thousand bakeries, where men, white with the dust of it, poured this flour into iron pans, to be shoved into the heat of iron ovens for bread to feed the nation. It is deplorable that the men of the Ne-con-dis, on the slopes of the Mis-sa-be, didn't stop for a moment, wipe the sweat from their faces, drop their iron picks and iron shovels—and listen. They'd have heard this growth of the soil, and the food fashioned from it, go roaring along the iron tracks of the Northern Pacific and the Chicago and Northwestern; farther south and east, day and night the steel rails of the New York Central and the great Pennsylvania screamed and whined under the steel wheels of endless freight trains rolling over them— trains pulled by coughing, hoarsely barking locomotives that had, perforce, to be built of iron. Themselves diggers in the earth, the Merritts should have reflected, remembered that these hundred thousand locomotives were fed by coal dug out of the earth with iron picks, and by water pumped out of the ground through iron pipes by huge pumps made of iron. It would have been wise for Leonidas —who did have a strong geographic sense!—to have looked at the rivers, for up and down America, across the Mississippi and the Wild Missourai, the Ohio and the lazy, muddy River Platte, a thousand products made from iron hurtled over steel bridges fabricated by Andy Carnegie's iron-masters and his grimy puddlers of steel.

In their peculiar, parochial pride and self-sufficiency, the Merritt men would have done well to think of the new, tall American money-temples, whose shells and walls were brick and concrete, but whose ribs and bones were built of steel. Here myriads of money-making men were scheming, bartering, buying, selling—thinking up new uses for new products to be forged from iron ore. Iron, in short, was the framework of all human life now; into the life-saving steel of surgeons' knives went iron ore. Iron was the harbinger of death: into armor-plate for battleships, into the sinister, cylindrical walls of howitzers iron was now flowing to prepare the doom that was to come to ten million men before Lon Merritt died.

The frame of human life must rust; the wheels of the world must stop; civilization itself must die —without iron. In the face of the vast intricate machine of life, what were these Merritt iron men? But Leonidas never realized their littleness, never showed humility, as he dug, and swore, and sweat to try to uncover the treasure that an iron world must have—regardless.

II

"But, Mister Merritt, ye know—this here ca-an't be an iron mine!" So a broad-cheeked, light-eyed Cornishman from the Gogebic Iron Range, in Upper Michigan, protested to Leonidas. Immensely shrewd, experienced wrinkles were around this Cornishman's eyes, and a look told you he was nothing if not a practical man.

"And why can't it be a mine?" cried Lon, formidable as usual, out of joint with the fitness of things according to his custom, dressed as he was in that white coat and vest, topped off with the pith helmet made for the tropics. Lon glared at the Michigan miner, who was unquestionably competent; and he tugged at his sweeping mustaches, pulled at his goatee that made him look much more like some misplaced cavalry commander of the Civil War than like the leading mining magnate of the Northwest—which glory he was now perfectly sure was about to be his. Lon kicked impatiently at the pile of dark, reddish-blue rubble that lay at his feet —it was earth with a strange look, a peculiar texture to it. And the Cornishman kept looking at the

117

hole from which this reddish-blue dirt—undoubt-
edly iron ore—had come.

"But this ca-an't be a mine. It's got no hangin'
wall. An' wheer's yer foot wall—tell me that!" The
Cornishman peered down the hole. "No hangin'
wall—no foot wall—so yer mine ca-an't be a mine,
that's a-all there's about it!"

Lon Merritt was annoyed, and not gently. If the
smack of his huge fist on the Cornishman's chin, if
mere devastating physical force could have won his
argument, Leonidas might have convinced this ob-
stinate man. Lon's face grew redder, by reason of a
magnificently exercised self-restraint; for a moment he was speechless, then he pointed to the ore:

"But what do you call that there? You know it's
been assayed, runs 64, even 66 percent of iron,
good pure iron—iron that's mighty low in phosphorus. Bessemer iron, you know—and isn't that
what all the down-Lakes furnacemen are yelling
for? And look at it. Just look at all of it—"

Lon swept his arm over this clearing where they
stood, a few acres gouged out of the vast tangle
of the Mis-sa-be forest, it was—a curious, sudden
opening, cluttered with a jumble of uprooted pine
trees, hastily sawed-off stumps, logs, buckets with
windlasses, picks and scrapers, crowbars and long-
handled scoop shovels. Here and there were rudely
built cabins, and crudely contrived wooden shacks,

118

and everywhere in the dirt of the clearing—the only open space for twenty miles roundabout—were holes. The ground was pitted and pock-marked with holes that might have been shell-holes on a battlefield; and these pits were surrounded by bowlders, by heaps of yellow clay, by piles of gravel, and always by mounds of red stuff, reddish-blue, and heavy. It was a fantastic, fine, soft dirt that ran like dust between your fingers, that didn't come up in chunks out of the ground as real iron ore ought to do—but it was, for all that, iron. Such was the first mine on the Mis-sa-be; it was called the Mountain Iron; this was the spring of '91.

"Yes, but—Mister Merritt, how the devil are ye goin' to sink a sha-aft into this stuff? Wheer's yer granite, an' yer grin-stun"—which was Cornish for greenstone—"an' yer diarite? Ye told me they're way back up the hill there—away from this ore. An' wheer's yer sh-lates? Ye ain't found sh-lates? Then this here is no mine! So—though this stuff *may* be iron, ye just ca-an't mine it!" And the Cornishman went his way.

This was a blow that it was hard for the thick-chested leader of the Ne-con-dis to stand. The adverse opinion of white-collared experts—those despised "scientific squirts"—never bothered Leonidas much. Long after these exciting times, Lon bore witness, under oath, to a solemn committee of Con-

119

gressmen: "Then after the Mountain Iron Mine was opened . . . it began to attract attention, and almost all the eminent experts were up there. They came up there to look over that country, and went away, and condemned it; amongst others there was no less a man than Rattle, who has almost world-wide fame." Forgetting for a moment all heart-aches, with a guffaw, Lon loved to tell, in his last days, why Rattle had turned down the Mountain Iron. In Mexico, Bert Merritt had run on to Rat-tle, and asked him the reason for his adverse opinion. "If I had ever put my *hand* in that ore—" confessed the eminent man. "I have kicked myself ever since that I did not put my hand in that ore, and then I'd have known it was ore!"

But here were Cornishmen, real miners, men who'd been born, you might say, with picks in their hands and torches on their caps. Now these fellows, callous-handed, and with no more abstruse mineral education than Lon himself had, but practical, were giving these new Merritt diggings the go-by. The Cornishmen were experienced, were against mere book-knowledge as Lon himself was, were accus-tomed to peer at the enigmatical, rocky slope of a Michigan hill, and utter the ancient Cornish saw: "Where it is, there it is, and you cannot see any further into the ground than any of us, nor tell us where the ore is likely to occur."

But these chaps, who knew ore when they saw it, had seen Lon's iron, and turned him down. Yes, they would admit that this was really iron, lying so strangely, under the pine needles, under the clay and gravel. "But where are the veins of ore?" they kept asking Lon. "But this is nothin'—it's only what we call a blanket formation." They kept explaining to him that this ore, lying so shallow, so flat, must be nothing more than a "slop-over" from some ancient ore-body long since worn and weathered away, or from a real vein lying far away to the south. If this ore on the Mis-sa-be didn't slant down into the ground at a steep pitch, at a sharp angle to the surface, between walls of rock, why, it couldn't go deep, so they assured him. Down on the Marquette, the Menominee, the Gogebic iron ranges, in Michigan, all good iron existed in veins dipping deep down into the ground at high angles —and if this ore didn't lie deep, there was no chance at all it could lie wide enough to make up for its shallowness. And, worse luck, these Cornishmen were apparently right, for, as the geologist, H. V. Winchell, wrote: "Flat deposits of ore of any considerable purity were unknown in this country."

In Duluth, in Superior, in the whole country round the Head of the Lakes, the Merritts were more than ever laughing-stocks. Folks respected their terrific industry, but their judgment? Here they'd brought down iron, high grade, and Bessemer too—but it was iron nobody in the world knew how to get out of the ground. Who could sink a shaft into that soft stuff—and even if somebody succeeded, with constant danger of deadly cave-ins, how far down did the iron go? In the clearing at Mountain Iron on the Mis-sa-be, windlasses creaked, and the various Merritts laughed, and swore, as they disappeared below ground in the buckets. Lon Merritt went on digging his holes.

"One man's theory is every bit as damn' good as another's—till it's busted," said Lon. And round their camp-fire council the Merritts made medicine once more, with Leonidas using his imagination to refute obvious and embarrassing facts. Out of his disappointments, his hopes of twenty-five years, his father Lewis's visions, out of the magnetic surveys of Cassius and John E., and because of his own utter disregard and igorance of where textbooks said iron should be found, Lon now evolved an iron-theory of his own. Crudely, across "Lon Merritt's New Sectional Map of the Mineral District of Northern Minnesota, 1890," Leonidas scrawled a weird, wavy line in red ink—a line thick in some places and thin in others. It was a mark that extended from a point west of the Mississippi, across St. Louis County, across the still largely unsurveyed Lake County, till it lost itself at last in the watery jungle beyond the boundary in Canada. This red, snaky line crawled northeast, always just south of the Height of Land, below the crest of the Mis-sa-be Heights, following the line of maximum magnetic attraction that had been plotted so laboriously by Cassius and John E.—and geologists today would find it interesting to compare with their modern maps, that show the exact trend of what's now called the famous Biwabik, or iron-bearing formation.

"Now—the way this ore lays," Leonidas told Alfred, Cassius, Johnnie, and the rest of them, "you can best describe it if you'd imagine a lake filled with water, with ordinary banks, and displace that water, and place into it—soft ore! And the ore lays in *basins,* just as water would lay in a lake —that's why it's flat," said Leonidas, in triumph.

And now, all along this red line on Lon's map, up and down the Mis-sa-be, with a vast imprudence, the men of the Ne-con-dis began to buy ore basins —that existed, alas, in their imaginations. "The Merritt family saw this thing big, from the start," said Alfred, though the way that silent man muttered through his drooping mustache you'd hardly accuse him of sharing the sweep of Lon's fantastic dreams. In the Minnesota legislature, Leonidas busied himself at lobbying, not by money, because he had next to none of it, but by friendliness, ca-

123

jolery, powerful argument. "I conceived the idea of the State passing a lease law, so this land could be taken up by comparatively poor people, and not be bought up at $5 or $10 an acre by some rich syndicate," said Lon. Such was his old-fashioned Americanism; and the very day the legislative session ended, the law was shoved through. State lands were now opened up, and all the way along Lon's red line on the map, from Bowstring on the west as far east as Gunflint Lake, the Merritts now made filings—on better than two hundred claims.

"Whatever money we could raise, whatever stuff we could sell," explained Leonidas, "we bought these basins with. We put in everything we ever made, and ever had."

So this imprudent, sanguine, and utterly unjustifiably optimistic band of brothers, with the communism of a tribe of Indians, risked the fruits of their life-work of pine-land-looking, in what you'd swear could only be a colossal silliness of speculation. Meanwhile, holes multiplied on that little clearing in Section 3 of Township 58, Range 18 West of the Fourth Principal Meridian—called Mountain Iron. Amid the creaking of windlasses and the screech of shovels on gravel, to the tune of the shouts, curses, laughter of now forgotten and always anonymous men, the test-pits grew so numerous that they ran into each other, coalesced, and around them all lay piles of red-blue, heavy ore—Bessemer. It was unprecedented: for the Merritt boys were turning up iron, not by the foot, but by the hundred yards.

III

JOHN E. MERRITT, the same who'd got himself so nearly lost for good on the Mis-sa-be back in '84, walked out of the Duluth office of his Uncle Leonidas, on air. And why shouldn't he now be proud, for Lon had just given him an official slip of paper —most important. "You realize, my boy," said Lon, "now you're General Manager of the Biwabik Mountain Iron Company, and everything is absolutely up to you!"

John E. was just thirty, and not at all in build like the squat, barrel-shaped Leonidas, but slender. A queer choice for mine manager in the rough Missa-be country you'd certainly have called this stripling, at first sight; for there was no aggressiveness to his wispy, rather droopy mustache; and in his mild, gray eyes it was hard to find anything else but kindness. The hair on top of his head was already scanty, and entirely gone in front: worn away, it had been, by years of rubbing of the misery-straps of the countless packs he'd toted through the northern bush. Still, the formidable Leonidas and his young nephew had this in com-

126

THE MOUNTAIN IRON CLEARING. X MARKS FIRST PIT IN IRON ON MISSABE RANGE

"JOHN E. WAS JUST THIRTY. . . . THERE WAS NO AGGRESSIVENESS IN HIS WISPY, RATHER DROOPY MUSTACHE"

mon: that the two of them were by all odds the most poetical of the Merritt clan. Lon, it is true, wrote, talked, thought, in the epic manner; his experiences were each and every one of them battles, and his business ventures had for their goals commercial empires, no less. John E.'s poetry was peculiarly that of the humble voyageur; it was romantic in a smaller way, and it told of the sufferings, the buffooneries, the small triumphs of woods-cruisers; his most glowing yarns were those of forest fires he'd barely escaped from; his most cherished memories were of generally forgotten self-sacrifices shown—in a crisis—by some plain bushwhacker for his anonymous comrade.* John's ears were never attuned to the jingle of dollars or the clangor of an iron America, but there was never a cruiser who could distinguish more subtly the comforting croon of the north wind in the white pines from its ghostly moan in the Norways. For the rest, he believed in his Uncle Leonidas, blindly, absolutely.

The only thing at all important about the Biwabik Mountain Iron Company, when John E. took hold of it, was its name. It had, this spring of '91, no mountain of iron that anybody knew of; in its treasury there was not a soo-markee, as Alf used to say; its assets were State lease lands that were valuable if—if Lon's theories about those iron-

* See Appendix E, page 222.

127

basins were right. To get money for blasting-powder, for grub, and to pay his men, our young manager tried to sell Biwabik stock, whose par was $100, for $10 a share, on time payments. "View my disappointment," he later confessed, "when the businessmen of Duluth turned me down with one accord. They did not hesitate to tell me that I was chasing the fabled pot of gold at the foot of my dream rainbow." Of course nobody would imagine a Duluth businessman of those rough days saying just that, but such, just the same, is John E.'s gentle remembrance of his failure. But who of the Merritts dared to face Leonidas, admitting failure?

"Next," wrote John, "I went to personal friends, who, because they loved me, were willing to gamble a little on this venture."

Presently this scanty-haired, frank-faced stripling tumbles, with the rest of his new mine-gang, off the Duluth and Iron Range train, eighty miles north of Duluth at Mesaba Station, east of Embarrass River. Here is a crew fit for any adventure: the strapping Wilbur Merritt is along, as Captain, and he's a gang in himself; the bushwhackers Wheeler, Culbertson, and Verne Richardson are there, and two of the younger Merritts—Alva and John J.

Alva, who is John E.'s brother, is only fifteen,

128

but already his muscles are knotty. Finally, along with a clatter of tin dishes, pots, kettles, comes the cook, Mr. Housell—who should certainly not be forgotten because of the fortune he made, and fantastically kept, as a result of this adventure. All these were loyal, were gamblers, were willing to take $20 of their $40 per month of pay, in money— and the rest in stock of the Biwabik.

The next day they broke the northern record for camp-building. They toted their irons for the buckets and windlass, the steel for their drills, their forge, striking hammers, picks and shovels along with them to the corner of Section 22 in Town 59, Range 14—it was near Lon's red line, but thirty miles east of Mountain Iron where ore was really in sight. In a day these heirs to Paul Bunyan had actually built an entire camp—a house of 26 by 24 feet, with double floor, double walls, double roof, and lined with tar paper. That day, in moments while he rested from his responsibility as General Manager, John E., himself, dug a well ten feet deep. Wheeler set up a blacksmith shop, and toward evening all brought in great heaps of balsam boughs for their beds. "By eleven o'clock that first night," wrote John E., "we were all asleep, and slept like tired healthy men call sleep." All excepting Wilbur: this indefatigable man stayed up past midnight, to finish the benches for the table, and along the bunks. For the next three months they dug, drilled, and blasted there, and struck— water.

The last night of that three months they were down in the mouth; the next morning they were up early, and singing, and started west on a thirty mile trek with their battered tools and dirty duffle to Section 8, of Town 58, Range 18. "We owned the fee of that," said John, "and it looked good because of the float ore on the surface, and because of its nearness to Mountain Iron." They dug there and failed again, still more miserably, so what good was this stock of the Biwabik Mountain Iron Company? But then came John E.'s strange chance meeting with the famous northern voyageur, John McCaskill—and now surely the fortunes of the lot of them were going to be made. The exact time and place of this encounter is in dispute: Alva Merritt will have it that his brother John met McCaskill on the streets of Duluth, while the Biwabik manager himself relates that this momentous meeting took place in the heart of the Mis-sa-be forest—but what matter? It is close enough to the truth to say that, after they'd failed at their second diggings, with their ardor not nearly so hot—and who blames them?—John E. and the giant Wilbur were stumbling west along the old Town Line Trail, back into the bush again after a discouraged trip to Duluth.

"Hey, boys! What luck?" It was McCaskill the Canadian, a man who was sharp-eyed, honest, supremely competent in the woods, regrettably a drunkard, but as an explorer hardly second to Cassius Merritt himself. The three of them writhe themselves out of their pack-sack straps, light their pipes and sit down to chew the fat. "Boys," says McCaskill, "when you get to the corner of Section 3, Town 58, Range 16—just drop your packs in the trail, an' go south a hundred paces or so—"

"But—that ain't our land. We ain't got the fee, nor even the lease of that piece!"

"No," said McCaskill, "John McKinley's got the handlin' of that land. But look here, I happened on to a pine tree there—up-rooted, it was, by that last big wind. Here's why I'm tellin' you about it. I can't deal with McKinley the way you can. But if what you see on the roots of that there tree looks good to you—I'll get an interest. Go to it!"

They knock out their pipes; their misery straps are in place on their foreheads once more; shaking hands, the three of them call a "so-long!" The cruiser McCaskill swings off toward the east, his lunging body merges into a tangle of cedar, of alder; his voyageur's song grows fainter, fainter.

131

Wilbur and John E. trudge west; lifted along by an unreasonable hope, they wallow through swamps of tamarack, grunt up and over windfalls, walk with their woodsmen's easy balance across a little tree that's the only bridge over rushing white water. And they stand—it seems no time—on the afternoon of this same day before John McCaskill's fallen pine tree. Down go their packs. Never would you catch such men as John E. and Wilbur leaving *their* packs in the trail, as McCaskill had told them to. "No good woodsman leaves his home and goes wandering about without it, besides, if this looked right to us, we did not care to have some one come along the trail and wait to inquire what had called us off on such an errand," wrote John E. Now the two of them dig, claw away at the leaves, branches, and rubble of little bushes with which McCaskill has craftily covered his mysterious tree. On the roots of this upturned ancient giant pine, plain though the shadows are falling, there glistens a yellow-red ocherous stain—"the red stain of the iron that had nourished it all the centuries it had stood there," so John E. put it. Dusk fell. The two of them kept rooting around, intent as a pair of extremely eager dogs. "We kept up our search. It looked good to us—wonderful. We found another old tree upturned, and there, under the débris of years, we again found ore. It looked—wonderful!"

A faith filled them: they never asked themselves how deep this ocher might go, whether it might get richer, redder and heavier should they dig downward. But here was, without doubt, the top of another one of Lon's basins! Cunningly covering their tracks they slipped back onto the trail, turned back east, toward the railroad, toward Duluth, toward Leonidas. They stumbled forward; their thighs ached; there were splints on their shins, knots in their calves. John E. slipped, grabbed at a tree, which snapped and let him down flat on his face, pack-sack on top of him. He got up, plodded on. "You catch at 'em," he growled to Wilbur, "thinkin' they're live ones—an' damn' if they ain't dead buggers, every time!" They laughed, and slogged forward—

But next morning, alas, in Duluth, the all-powerful Uncle Leonidas wasn't to be found; called away, he had been, on one of his incredibly numerous activities. And McKinley? That canny man—though he knew absolutely nothing about the value of his little piece of land by the uprooted pine in Section 3-58-16—on general business principles wanted all the dough in the world for it. John E. was rattled; for, though dauntless in the bush, bargaining was no part of his business in life. He was the youngster that Leonidas could bank on, to leave his young wife who had two days before

133

that borne her first baby, to go off up on the range never seeing his dear ones at all, nor even hearing from them—until six weeks later. But in a bargain John E. was, maybe, a bit gentle. So, for lack of Leonidas, he called in Cassius, and together with that incomparable Merritt cruiser he begged, haggled, traded, and expostulated with McKinley. McKinley laughed in their faces, was haughty, asked sixty thousand dollars for the fee of his property, in addition to a royalty of twenty-five cents per ton on the ore from it—providing there *was* ore —and he would give them only a miserable ten days' option in which to explore, before they'd have to plank down the money. Disheartened, they left him; shrewdly they went to a bank, discovered McKinley owed heavily there, overdue; that night Cassius and John E. went to bed, limp, with the bargain closed at thirty thousand dollars, no royalty. But, alas, with only ten short days to find out whether this Godforgotten little corner of the Missa-be forest was worth paying ten cents for. Not a day more than ten—and here was a day gone already—

IV

"Now don't you fellows worry—I'll get our whole Biwabik outfit away from 8-58-18, and land 'em for you by the new location—noon, tomorrow!"

"But, Wilbur," said John E., "they're better'n thirty miles west of here—an' they're twenty miles west of McCaskill's diggings. . . ."

"All right—the trip'll be good for my health. Y' see—I need the exercise," and Wilbur executed a buffoonish lumberjack's fandango. Such was this barge of a slab-sided Merritt, who'd first known his strength on that so nearly tragic day, years before, when he'd carried his helpless Uncle Cashie over the featherbed swamp near the Whiteface River. It was now five in the evening of the second day of John E.'s option, after his exceedingly risky bargain with McKinley. Together with John E. and Captain Nicols, Wilbur shoveled in a frontiersman's supper at old Frank Schurz's place at Mesaba Station. Wilbur pulled at his belt, heaved his shoulders. "The walk'd be a bit tough for you, at your age, Captain," said Wilbur, with respect, to old Nicols. "So I'll just meet you and Johnnie at

3-58-16, noon, tomorrow." And he was off toward Mountain Iron, in the cool, long twilight of that northern August evening, due west over the twisting, intricate Town Line trail that was hardly more than a vague indication of a path, and no road at all. By three the next morning Wilbur was hammering at the door of the Mountain Iron Camp— thirty miles west of where he started. "Get up, Blois, an' hitch your horses, right off. Big doin's— Johnnie's movin' the Biwabik outfit again."

Poor Blois grunted, cursed feebly. "Wha-a-t—"

"No *what* about it, me b'y. Shake a leg! Drive your team over to 8-58-18 right away, an' wake up the Biwabik boys there—an' load the whole outfit —leavin' Alvie to watch the camp. We got to begin test-pitting on 3-58-16 by noon, today—"

Blois struggled into his shoe-pacs, growled it was five miles from here to the old camp, and at least twenty from there to the new diggings, that it was impossible, that it was—

"You shake a leg!" roared Wilbur. "We got something this time—but McKinley's only givin' us ten days to find out whether we got something or no. You *got* to make it!"

For just one hour, no more, no less, Wilbur lay down to rest. That day, at noon, Blois, Wilbur, the team, the Biwabik men and their duffle, the buckets and windlasses, the striking hammers, the cook-

136

stove and its priest, Mr. Housell, were cluttered
about McCaskill's mysterious upturned tree. By a
cunning blind trail they'd carted everything in,
over a crafty road brushed out that morning by
John E. and Nicols, a path that led out from the
tree, but stopped short of the main tote road—nobody's business what the Merritts were up to, now.
The stove was set up and the noon meal cooked by
the shrewd and fortunate Mr. Housell, and by one
o'clock of the afternoon of that day the cross-cut
saws were buzzing into white pines, axes were thud-
ding against the tangle of bushes, trees were top-
pling over amid shouts and with rending booming
crashes, shovels were shrieking on gravel, bowlders
were being sworn at, bellowed at, and rolled out of
their ancient beds by straining, red-faced, grunting
men. "Close by McCaskill's tree, where we first saw
signs of iron beneath its roots," said General Manager John E. Merritt, "we started Pit Number One
of the Biwabik Mine."

Day and night, for seven days and seven nights,
Manager John E. and Captain Wilbur and their
Biwabik gang, dug holes. In an absolute, sweating,
toiling, frenzied communism, in an excitement of
discovery, where the men cursed at the bosses and
the bosses shoveled harder than their helpers, they
dug deep holes on this curious southern slope of the
Mis-sa-be hills, where the ancient Continental ice-

cap, for reasons of its own, had neglected to deposit a thick layer of clay and gravel.

In the lovely dawn 'mid the drone and the maddening whine of a billion bloodthirsty mosquitoes they dug—oblivious; at high noon, in the blaze of a sun they had a right to call tropical, they shoveled, never feeling the bites of the ferocious black-flies whose stabs drew blood that they wiped into grotesque streaks on their sweaty faces; in cold midnights under the eerie flare of torches that drove the shadows back and back into the surrounding pines, they bent their backs, harder, harder, at the handles of the windlasses—and never knew the nights were cold.

The whites of their eyes turned a bloodshot red, and yet they seemed to need no sleep; when their bellies gnawed at them in nature's insistent proclamation of hunger, they ate, wolfishly, not knowing what they ate at all; and, wiping their mustaches with the backs of their hands, they hurled themselves at their shovels, picks, and windlass handles. The shrieks of these machines—that cried for oil which one and all of this maddened crew were too busy to give them—mingled with curses, with laughter, with exultant cries. For the pits drove down, through negligible glacial gravel—to ore, iron ore, first yellow and ocherous, then brown, now red and heavy, till at last the walls of these holes gleamed, in the torchlight, a deep, a magically sparkling, fantastic blue—

They dug in a dream, this John E. and his men, not believing their eyes, driving down pit after pit over a huge plot of what three days before had been virgin forest. Three, six, nine, ten pits they gouged out till even their tough hands were blistered, and bled. And all they had to do was to lift out iron, iron—just a few feet of gravel, a thin layer of paint-rock you didn't have to blast, and it was incredible how in every pit all over the place they struck pure iron ore. Here, at last, toward the end of that frantic week of labor, was the famous Pit No. 11; it went fifty feet down and was bottomed in ore, lustrous blue, and heavy; for all they knew the ore in this pit might reach down to China. At the end of their week they had uncovered an area of five hundred by five hundred and fifty feet—all ore; all traditions were smashed, for here was ore, not by the foot, or the hundred yards, but by the acre. Who would laugh at Lon Merritt's ore basins now?

The day of the tenth and last day of the option, John E., not quite sane, and looking out through red-rimmed eyes at a world that seemed not quite real, jumped off the train at Duluth. To Lon he went, and quickly that chieftain called a council, with Alfred the silent businessman, with Cassius,

the explorer. John E. had no time to think of his
young wife, his baby; through cracked lips in husky
whispers the young discoverer told his three uncles
of the millions, the unbelievable myriads of tons of
high-grade iron ore he'd opened up on the Biwabik.
"And sure Uncle Cashie's told you I took that option—entirely on my own responsibility," he said
to Lon and Alf. "And you realize the Biwabik
Mountain Iron Company can have the whole thing,
the *fee* of it—for only thirty thousand dollars!"

Such was the strange, communistic faith of one
Merritt in the word of another that they never questioned him; hurriedly Lon went to the capitalist,
K. D. Chase, to other prudent moneyed men who
had invested along with them in the Biwabik Company. But these sane men balked, said the company
had enough land already, made the sagacious re-
mark that thirty thousand dollars was—well, thirty
thousand dollars; and they propounded the old
poser: "How're you goin' to mine it—layin' flat
like you say it does?" And they plainly stated their
indignation at this unbusinesslike procedure of
Lon's letting a whippersnapper like John have the
promise of such vast funds at his disposal. They
tried to pour cold water down the spine of the enthusiastic Leonidas: "If you make this purchase, it
must be on you Merritt boys' own responsibility,

without loss to us!" But they did not flabbergast the chief of the Ne-con-dis.

Together Lon and Alf "scurried around," as Alf liked to put it, and borrowed the money, and paid McKinley. On their own credit as Merritt boys they raised it—and that credit was next to unlimited in the State of Minnesota, since those old days when they'd piled their schooner *Chaska* on the rocks, and sawed logs in the woods till they'd paid every cent of their $1,500 indebtedness. They bought McKinley's land in 3-58-16; they might have kept it for themselves; like the simple square-shooters that they were, they added it to the holdings of the Biwabik Mountain Iron Company.

At the same time these optimists found a way, that was simple, practical, and entirely new, of getting this flat-lying ore out of their basins at Mountain Iron and Biwabik. "We don't have to mine it!" cried John E., or Alf, or Lon, or Cassius, or Wilbur—there's now no record of just which one of the Ne-con-dis had this hunch. "All we've got to do is to *shovel* off that over-burden of gravel— and there's our ore, right in a stock-pile!" They thought first of using horse-drawn scrapers, and wagons; but they were Americans, with Americans' mania for speed, for large-scale operations; in the wink of an eye their thoughts went to that most typical American tool: "Why—this is nothin' but a steam-shovel proposition; it's just a contractor's job—that's all!" At a jump they cleared all the objections of Cornishmen, of expert miners, not by genius, but by horse-sense. There'd be no expensive, deep shafts on the Mountain Iron or the Biwabik, no timbering, no costly air-pumps nor air-compressors. They were simply going to scoop out great open holes, open pits where men would shovel out ore with next to no hazard, in the daylight under the open sky.

"Why—we're going to mine this ore for next to nothing a ton, for labor! Why—it'll revolutionize—"

PART FOUR

FUGATO

"Probably the most generous people in the world are the very poor, who assume each other's burdens in the crises which come so often to the hard-pressed."

JOHN D. ROCKEFELLER

"And I understand woodcraft a great deal better than I do anything else."

LEONIDAS MERRITT

I

"CARNEGIE sent a man up there," said Leonidas Merritt, "and he took samples of that ore, which he showed me, and they ran well. They showed us the assays, and they were good."

The Merritt boys had cooked up the grand, cheap, original scheme of scooping the ore out of their basins with steam-shovels—but even Lon, Alfred, Wilbur, and Cassius couldn't carry steam-shovels into the Mis-sa-be woods on their backs. Now if only they'd been a wee bit patient, they wouldn't have had to carry any more loads, whatever—

"Then I had an interview with Frick—" Leonidas continued—

The accurate Bridge, in his *Inside History of the Carnegie Steel Company,* tells of the events, absolutely momentous for America, that Frick was brewing, scheming:

"In the Consolidation of July 1st, 1892, the Carnegie Steel Company, Limited, became owner of the Upper and Lower Union Mills, the Lucy Furnaces, the Edgar Thomson Steel Works, the newly acquired property at Duquesne, the Keystone Bridge Works, with a few other interests in ore and natural gas sprinkled about Western Pennsylvania."

The steely-eyed steelmaster, Henry Clay Frick, had everything now, from blast furnaces to rolling mills, everything—excepting what was most needful of all: iron ore. For the Carnegie ore mines round Tyrone, Pennsylvania, had proved a costly failure, had been one of those misadventures that made the jovial Andy Carnegie write: "Pioneering don't pay." Now Frick had two passions, in his pre-art-lover days: he must make more and more millions of good steel ingots for American bridges, bathrooms, skyscrapers, plows and harvesters, baby-buggies, and steel rails;but better yet, he must make the making of them—pay. But to bring that about, to send Andrew Carnegie's profits shooting skywards even while the selling-price of steel rails went down, it wasn't enough for him simply to consolidate, to scrap million dollar plants, ruthlessly, to save twenty-five cents a ton on pig iron. Frick had to have ore, sure, cheap, unlimited—

Back in Duluth, Lon and Alf Merritt knew that their tremendous iron treasure might, for all the good it was doing them, or their beloved north country, as well be underground in Timbuctoo—so

146

long as there were no rails to get it down to Lake Superior.

"I had a talk with Frick—" said Leonidas. Frick, of course, could do anything. To connect up his roaring, flame-spouting forges and rolling mills that were turning America from a sprawl of over-grown country villages into a world-power, he'd built the famous Union Railroad. It was a master-stroke; it ran all around and through the lurid, grimy, useful Pittsburgh district; the saving to Car-negie on the switching charges alone paid the inter-est on its cost; it rebated the murderously expensive ore-carrying rates by twenty-five cents a ton. All because the cold-eyed, bearded titan, Frick, had racked his brains in a grim intensity, of down-with-costs, cut-costs, slash-costs.

Back at the Head of the Lakes, Alf Merritt knew better than anybody that their bonanzas at Mountain Iron, and Biwabik, might as well be sleeping under the pine-needles and glacial gravel —unless he could turn the red-blue streams of the ore of them from the Mis-sa-be down into the Alle-gheny furnaces. Even Alf was impatient.

The phenomenally growing steel framework of our country, the Carnegie Company, and Henry Frick, lacked—ore. "This," wrote the thorough historian, Bridge, "was the only thing the Carnegie Company had to buy of outsiders. So long as it did

147

not itself produce everything it needed, it could not be considered a perfect industrial unit."

Leonidas, in his sworn testimony before the Congressional Committee on Investigation of the United States Steel Corporation, said: "I had an interview with Frick. . . . Frick did not use me like a gentleman, and cut me off short, and bulldozed me—"

II

"When Uncle Lon got to writing one of his poems," said Alva Merritt, "he went at it just like everything else, kept at it, day and night, for a couple of days—and then like as not he'd sleep for twenty-four hours."

Frick had failed him, but the Merritt boys couldn't carry steam-shovels up there on their backs, not even Wilbur. They must have a railroad. So Leonidas, the bushwhacker, spat upon his hands and sat himself down to write a poem.* "A Lay of the Mis-sa-be" he called it; and it was written with a crude strength but still in the manner of the gentle Longfellow who had first made Kitchi Gammi famous. In it Lon proceeded to entertain, to admonish, to beg, and to plead with the reluctant citizens of the Head of the Lakes—not to turn down the wealth that lay ready for them back of the gabbro hill. Alone in his office, at midnight, in that curious room hung with snow-shoes, cluttered with lumberjacks' mementoes, Lon drove his pen over endless sheets of foolscap—

* See Appendix H, page 228.

". . . Something of its old traditions,
Something of its growing future
And the aye to make it brighter—
If you'll ask me I will tell you."

It began as vivid geography, proving Lon's contention that Duluth was the Zenith City, the real hub of America; it turned into a saga of that battle with thicket, snow, and hunger that Stuntz, his own father, and all the Merritts had fought; it yelled defiance against the down-lakes prosperity of Chicago; it celebrated the Merritt boys' discovery of the Mis-sa-be Iron Range; it was, finally and chiefly, a booster's exhortation fit to draw first prize in a modern Rotary Club—

"We are going to build a railway,
With easy grades for transportation,
From the mines of the Mis-sa-be
To the smokestacks of the Zenith,
To the furnaces for smelting,
To the mills where cunning fingers
Fashion articles for commerce,
Structural steel and heavy castings,
Tools and rails and nails and whatnot."

Why shouldn't Leonidas throw all of his energy, his fury of utterance, into making his skeptical fellow-citizens loosen up for a railroad? From all over America, experts were flocking to the Mis-sa-be, this time to stay. At the Biwabik, with young

John E. proudly presiding, great whales of the American iron-mining industry disappeared below ground down the test-pits in buckets. Pick in hand D. H. Bacon, W. J. Rattle, the geologist H. V. Winchell, H. M. Curry, J. A. Crowell, and the famous Johnny Jones, were lowered in iron-hooped barrels. They scraped deep grooves out of the pit-walls as they went down, letting the gleaming strange earth run into their buckets as they descended—from hard layers, from soft, from sand-streaks and all. The ore they brought up was red, blue, purple, brown, green, black—but it was as remarkably uniform in its analysis for iron as it was variable in its glittering hues and plays of color. Pit Number 15 yielded that marvelous sample which ran 67.9 percent for iron, only 1.8 percent in silica—with a negligible 0.016 percent of phosphorus that made it Bessemer equal to the best ores from the Vermilion. Experts, with red dust still on their shoes, stumbled through the woods to Mesaba Station; with red-stained fingers they filed mysterious telegrams, in code, to iron-masters, capitalists, down the Lakes.

Right away they must have a railroad; and Lon begged the frugal bankers, merchants, small capitalists of Duluth, who believed completely in the Merritt credit, but were—alas—so doubtful of the Merritts' optimistic dreams:

151

"Put some cash in the Mis-sa-be,
Lend a helping hand to others,
Others who are working for you.
Let us bind with bands of iron
The Mis-sa-be to the Zenith—"

Lon and Alf had already tried to get the St.
Paul and Duluth Railroad to build in to Mountain
Iron—but President Plough wouldn't hear of it;
and the officials of the Northern Pacific, too, had
turned them down with apologetic smiles. At last,
one hectic hopeful evening at the Merchant's Hotel
in St. Paul, Leonidas and Alfred incorporated the
Duluth, Mis-sa-be, and Northern Railroad. Their
associates were K. D. Chase and his brother from
Faribault, the gigantic Donald Grant, and Messrs.
Guthrie and Foley. They had ore; they had land;
they had everything—but money.

Meanwhile, transformations you might almost
call geological shook the ancient pine forest of the
Mis-sa-be to its roots, slashed, gouged, demolished
it. Duluth businessmen woke up at last, went after
iron on their own hooks: Judge J. T. Hale, A. E.
Humphreys, and George Milligan and many others
were sending grubbers in now with picks and
shovels; their exultant, hopeful and profane bellow-
ings smashed what ten years before you would have
called the eternal silences of the Mis-sa-be forest.
The famous Frank Hibbing came, and the ex-

tremely able Captain Joseph Seilwood—but the Merritts were ahead of everybody.

At their orginal location at Mountain Iron, the illustrious Cornishman Captain Gill scratched off the earth's clay-gravel skin and disclosed a raw red tissue of pure iron. That burly man and his reckless men widened the first little clearing in a gargantuan fury of chopping, blasting, digging, loading, and hauling away. His broad candid face was illumined by mild gray eyes that looked innocent but had seen everything. He worked like the devil himself, and, putting twice too much dynamite under a stump, sent that sawed-off remnant of a giant pine up into the air and crashing horribly through the roof of the cook-shanty where his own good wife at this very moment was getting dinner for the workmen. Gill rushed into the ruin, mad with worry, to help, to comfort her. On the floor she writhed, with a broken hip, and in her pain she cried aloud. But when Gill found out that her hurt was surely not mortal, he straightened up, he smiled. He told her: "Ah—mother, but it was a mighty fine bla-a-ast!"

Nevertheless, civilization came to Mountain Iron, led by the Merritts. Roscoe, brother of the formidable Wilbur, floundered along the tote-road in March of '91, encouraged by the "sweet-sweet—bitter!" of innumerable song sparrows. Starting from Mesaba Station, Roscoe tucked his boots into his trouser-tops, skated, slid, careened, and stumbled over the yellow, sticky surface of that infamous road that wound through the woods between high banks of softening snow. He arrived, so he said, "in due course of mud," and founded at Mountain Iron the first store on the Mis-sa-be Range. It cost him three times as much to tote his stock of merchandise the thirty miles from the railroad, as it would have cost him to ship the same amount from Duluth to Liverpool. Mobs of men, uncouth, avaricious, bold, and dangerous, swarmed here; and for their needs—because payrolls were fat and money flush, Lon started a bank, which had one room, but a magnificent sign, gilt letters on black. For forty miles along the Mis-sa-be ridge men staked claims, at random and helter-skelter; a few found ore. Alf and Lon, because of their experience, because of their fantastic basin theory that was turning out to be right—discovered new basins of iron.

In March of '92, while Johnny Jones was frantically writing and wiring to Furnaceman Peter Kimberly, of Sharon, that acres, literally acres of ore had been discovered on the Biwabik—the Merritts made their greatest find of all. Peter Kimberly was sure Johnny Jones had gone crazy, and came north to get him properly put in a sanitarium, but discovered that, instead of there being forty acres of ore, as Johnnie had said—there were better than eighty at Biwabik. While Peter Kimberly was rubbing his eyes, Leonidas gave certain secret instructions to his man, Captain J. G. Cohoe, who sneaked east from Mountain Iron—many would have given thousands to know where Lon sent him, such was the Merritt name for luck, for knowledge. Cohoe stuck in his shovel on State Lease Land in the Northeast Quarter of Section 8, Town 58-17; it was fantastic when you remember that this was hardly two looks and a holler from that spot where John E. had got himself so nearly fatally lost, that snowy evening in November, '84,—on the momentous day when Uncle Cashie had found his first lean iron bowlder. Not so far from where John E.'s frightened feet had wandered, Cohoe sank his pit; first whack, fourteen feet down, he struck rich iron —under pine trees "whose roots," John E. liked to say, "were anchored in bands of iron." This started the greatest of the Merritt mines—the Mis-sa-be Mountain, which Lon in his booster's poem had called "that young giant of the future," not knowing how he'd understated its riches. Now the Merritts were kings of the range, were riding the crest; now Henry Frick must sit up and take notice. Here

155

was treasure to start the Ne-con-dis on a climb to limitless fortune; at last the Merritts had—arrived. Now, not as in the old fish and potato days to encourage themselves, but because the iron world was at their feet, they could, this spring of '92, whistle with the blackbirds and sing with the robins.

III

The learned geologist, H. V. Winchell, in 1892, at the close of those first two exciting years whose principal discoveries were the Mountain Iron, the Mis-sa-be Mountain, the Biwabik, wrote: "More merchantable ore is already known to exist on the Mesabi Range than has been produced from all the other mines in the Lake Superior Region since they were first discovered."

In regard to the true priority of discovery, in his *Report on the Mesabi Iron Range,* Winchell stated this fact: "The Merritt brothers, of Duluth and Oneota, were not to be discouraged by reports of explorers and miners added to those of experts and geologists who had condemned the range ever since 1875. To these Duluth pioneers the Mesabi was an attractive and promising district and their faith in it was never shaken. To them belongs the credit for persisting in the hunt for ore and the final discovery of it. . . ."

To become sensational American successes, to be nabobs of the Northwest second only to Jim Hill himself, all that Alfred and Leonidas now had to do was to sit back—and wait—

But, in the summer of '91, you see three men struggling over that wooded, wild, and water-logged plain that stretched from the Mis-sa-be Heights toward the edge of the gabbro hill at Duluth. They are Cassius C. and Wilbur J. Merritt, along with old Tom Sandelands, who is a kind of cousin, who is Scotch as haggis, who as an explorer can show both of them tricks. In the lobby of the Spaulding Hotel at Duluth there's a red-faced, wilt-collared seething of frenzied financiers who are incorporating mining companies to a value of more than five millions of dollars every day. Meanwhile, Tom, Wilbur, and Cassius blaze the trail for the new railroad—they are equipped with nothing but their axes and a pocket compass, plus a knowledge of that blank, mysterious, totally un-inhabited tangle that is unique, incomparable; for Wilbur and Cassius, to say nothing of Sandelands, had been lost all over that country! This is the very land out of which Wilbur carried the crippled Cassius on that so nearly tragic land-looking journey of the middle 'eighties—when they were still unknown. But now they're part of the notorious, the lucky, the envied clan of the Merritts, and full of confidence they're at their job of making the preliminary survey for the railroad that's going to

158

release an unparalleled flood of iron ore toward the furnaces at the foot of the Lakes.

Everything is now breaking right for the Merritts; even Nature who has cheated them so often is kind now. On this elevated plateau where Cashie squints, judges, cuts notches in trees, remote, prehistoric, terrific events had prepared an extraordinary path for iron to roll down toward Lake Superior's rim. Of course, Cassius and Wilbur didn't philosophize about that, didn't even know it, as they plodded intently at their job of running a line, on the gentlest possible down-grade, with the fewest possible cuts and fills, across the minimum number of rivers and creeks, from Mountain Iron toward the St. Louis River. But, over this peculiar plain, the mischievous, capricious, and awful Continental ice-cap had, in remote days, crawled with majestic slowness out of the North in successions of centuries when the snow never had a chance to melt for a thousand summers. Tom Sandelands was close-fisted with himself, free in lumberjack's fashion with his friends, and when not vastly drunk for weeks at a time, was practical; old shaggy Tom, second only to Lon Merritt himself when it came to sarcasm, and with a marvelous nose for direction, was probably incapable of even imagining how, in its dreadful, irresistible advance, the slowly moving mountain of ice had knocked the top off the Mis-

159

sa-be Range, had scattered frivolously, irretrievably, millions of tons of rich iron ore. Tom had biting, salty Scottish words for everybody excepting his adored Alf Merritt—Alf, in Tom's judgment, was the real leader of the Ne-con-dis, rather than the more spectacular Leonidas. Like Cassius, Tom had that peculiar sense of the master-explorer, which made him feel, in his back, his leg-muscles, the toil that future locomotives would have if the grade was not laid just so. But he didn't dream why, down from the Mis-sa-be, there was this marvelous, gentle levelness, this slight but continuous, convenient, down-hill. Mapping the easy route, Tom was oblivious to the way in which, ages before, the melting ice-cap had helped him. . . .

For, after completely hiding the Mis-sa-be Ridge during nobody knows what stretches of time, the summers had, for some inscrutable reason, become balmy again, and the rocks of the Mis-sa-be had begun to stick out—curious nunataks in a lonely, lifeless desolation of ice. This melt had been positively Providential, for, as the ice melted back toward the northwest and southeast, it left a great lake too between its fingers—a lake with a wonderfully level bottom of clay. So flat was the bed of this by-gone body of water that Tom and Cassius and Wilbur now could lay the line of the new railroad straight as an arrow across the muskegs for twenty-five miles. The grade slanted down toward Lake Superior so nicely that, if you gave a train of ore-laden cars a good start at the mines, they'd almost roll by themselves the fifty miles to the St. Louis River! The grade was down with the load, up with the empties—

So well did Cassius, Wilbur, and Tom Sandelands know this country, that the preliminary survey cost the new Duluth, Mis-sa-be, and Northern Railroad only five hundred dollars.

As for Alfred and Leonidas, anybody could at this moment have played a game of cards on their coat-tails, so energetically did they buzz back and forth and around from the Range to Duluth, from Duluth to St. Paul, and over to Faribault in their new game of being promoters, capitalists. With Minnesota magnates, with bankers of the northwest these two former bushwhackers now held up their end; Leonidas was hopeful, expostulatory; Alfred was sententious, but had the energy of a deep swift river. Alfred and Lon between them put ten thousand dollars, cash, into the new railroad, and owned one-fifth interest in this Duluth, Missa-be, and Northern. Together, without a doubt, they contributed five-fifths of the harebrained optimism, the faith to convert it from a mere grandiose plan on a blue-print into two parallel streaks of iron that reached toward the range from the Lake.

161

Together with the Chases, big Donald Grant and his brother, and Messrs. Guthrie and Foley, the Merritt boys raised fifty thousand dollars in cash—an amount of money not to be sneezed at in those times, and considering those ominous days of just before the '93 panic. Having failed with Frick, Lon remained confident, defiant, coined a new slogan, and told everybody:

"We'll make the Mis-sa-be and the railroad a Minnesota enterprise!"

But Duluth—alas—didn't want them. To the city council they went, asking for the right-of-way across the city streets for the new iron railroad. They were refused it. But nothing could stop them, and Lon and Alf, a few weeks after, contracted to link up their proposed railroad with the line of the Duluth and Winnipeg—which touched Lake Superior at the city of Superior, in Wisconsin, just across St. Louis Bay. For want of money, they used their wits. "We went at it," said Leonidas, "and employed Mr. Martz, whom I knew to be a good engineer, and a good woodsman, and an honest man, because I had had lots of deals with him before . . . and we built that road, about seventy miles." And Charley Martz, catching the virus of Lon's enthusiasm, turned gravel pits furnished him by the benevolent old glacier into roadbed; he built his construction camps out of the trees he had to

162

cut down to clear the right-of-way; timber cleared to make room for the roadbed served him for ties; wooded jungles faded away into bridges. When he needed money to pay the men, Lon and Alf raised it—on the strength of a now generally recognized enormous tonnage of iron in the Mountain Iron and Biwabik. As rapidly as in wartime emergency, and straight as a string, the railroad cut its gash through the bush toward the mines. It cost, as it melted the forest before it, the unbelievably small sum of ten thousand dollars per mile. Alf and Lon simply didn't have it in them to sit back and wait.

IV

"A JOLLY party of excursionists took a trip to Mountain Iron Saturday on the D. M. & N., given by the Merritt brothers in honor of their mother, Mrs. Hepzibeth Merritt, of Oneota, it being her eightieth birthday." So reports a Duluth newspaper of mid-October, 1892.

This is Hepzibeth's day, there's no doubt of it, and there's no doubt, too, that she has been a long time at her knitting, waiting for it. Today she is making her first journey to the Mis-sa-be Range, on one of the first trains to run over the Duluth, Mis-sa-be, and Northern Railroad—built by her sons. Today she will see the official, solemn, and formal opening of the Mountain Iron Mine—that her sons and grandsons have discovered. Hepzibeth weighs hardly more than a hundred pounds, but sharp eyes look out from her thin-lipped pioneer face that is still remarkably not wizened, nor very deeply wrinkled. Of course, in this excited picnic she is insignificant; she is lost, almost, in this noisy crowd of old-settler celebrants in Lon's handsome new passenger coach that still smells of paint and

164

"LEONIDAS . . . WHO LOOKED MORE LIKE A DRESSED-
UP BLACKSMITH THAN A POET"

"HEPZIBETH . . . HAS BEEN A LONG TIME AT HER
KNITTING"

varnish. See the folks, who've made the Head of
the Lakes, who are here today! The Duluth newspaper lists their names in three social castes, classes,
categories, as follows: "Prominent among the in-
vited guests"; and "The following Ladies and
Gentlemen"; and "The following from Superior,"
—which is not strange, for in those fiercely com-
petitive days many Duluthians would not admit
that Superior folks could be prominent, or ladies
and gentlemen. The new, slightly absurd little train
lurches and bounces, bangs and rattles over the not
yet settled roadbed. Its din is drowned in the chat-
ter, the unrestrained frontier laughter of the old
settlers, who make merry, on gallons of fresh milk
and abundant sandwiches—not dainty—supplied
them by the strictly teetotal Alfred and Leonidas.

Hepzibeth peers from the car windows at the
woods, and remembers: the gawdy reds and yellows
of the sumac and wild cherry are already fading—
so quick, so sad is this northern autumn. Well—life
is quick. . . . To Hepzibeth all this pother about
her, pride in her, honor for her, is a little incredible.
Why—it's like yesterday, but really it'll be thirty-
six years, a few days from now, that she herded this
brood of her boys on to that sidewheel steamer of
the forgotten name, whose mate was Big-Mouth
Charley, and delivered them safe to her man, Lewis
Merritt—who had the unfounded theory that there

was something marvelous up north here in these
uninhabitable woods. . . . Yesterday, a stretch of
poverty-stricken yesterdays, and now this: it can't
quite be true. And her eyes darken as she looks at
Leonidas bustling proudly up and down the aisle.
Watch out, Lonnie—you always *have* seen things
a little too big. . . . But here's Alf, close by her,
still for all his new importance looking no more than
the shrewd lumberjack that he is—ah, there's the
balance wheel of her strange gang of boys. Her
eyes brighten: Alfred will hold things down; he'll
nail down all they've discovered. And yet—are the
Merritts out of the woods at last? There is a mix-
ture of doubt, of reserved, stern pride in her eyes
as she gazes out at the swiftly passing tangle of
thicket that Lon, Alf, Cashie—her boys—have subdued. Her thoughts flit back over thirty short summers and thirty long winters of potatoes and fish,
fish and potatoes. Her eyes flash a little as she looks
at the weathered faces of her sons, at their burly
shoulders that always have a way of making their
clothes seem too small for them—well! They've
earned all this. . . . If they really have it.

But of course they've got it; their names are in
newspapers all over America. The train grates and
jars to a stop, around a curve of hastily laid rails
it would be more accurate to call part of a hexagon
rather than a curve. There's a bellow of "M-o-u-n—

t-i-n I—ern!" Her boys are men of the hour. Outside there's a boisterously respectful welter of
workmen to greet them, at the head of them the
faithful, the gigantic Captain Gill. The red stains
of iron are washed off their hands and faces—shin-
ing from unaccustomed soap and northern air; one
and all they're dolled up in their black Sunday
best; and as Leonidas lifts her down into the crowd
they let out a mighty yell. She blinks a bit. Why—
it's for her—it's for Grandma Merritt they're yelling these hoorahs! Slowly she walks, on the arm of
Alfred, toward a great mound of earth, strange,
enormous, at the foot of the clearing. "That's over-
burden, mother," mutters Alf. "Dirt we strip off
to get at our iron—that's all we have to do—"

They're quiet now, the whole crowd. Ceremonies
that have a rough dignity, solemnity, have begun
—and end with a short address by the Dominie, Dr.
Forbes, who extols Lon for his imagination, Alf
for his strength, his shrewdness, Cashie for his explorer's genius. Forbes has good words for all, for
the giant Wilbur, the brave, gentle John E., for
Lewis J. and the stern-faced Andrus, and old Napoleon, yes—and we mustn't forget the Reverend
Lucien—that bearded, upright man, whose exam-
ple has toughened the moral, the spiritual fiber of
the Merritt iron men. . . . "But you haven't seen
the mine, yet, mother," says Alfred. He picks her

up, in arms that have carried five times her weight, and more; slowly he carries her up the great mound of dirt, clay, gravel. Hepzibeth looks down into a weird man-made chasm whose walls gleam ocherous, dull red, and blue. . . . Who will dare to imagine her feelings now? For she sees it all. No, it is not a dream—this iron. Yes, it is her boys who have found it, are digging it, own it. . . . Her boys—

From the crowd massed below a voice comes up to her: "Three cheers for Grandma Merritt!"

There's a roar: "Hoo—ray! . . . Hoo—ray! . . . Hoo—ray!"

V

THE red-winged blackbirds have stopped their whistling and have already vanished from their swampy homes; the northern robins have finished their singing and are banding for the long flight south away from the cold that's coming; Alfred and Leonidas whistle, hum, and are happy, and who would deny they've a right to be? It's the day after Grandma Merritt's triumph; it's the occasion of the very first car of iron ore ever shipped from the Mis-sa-be, starting down toward the Lake. In the Mountain Iron open-pit the engineers of the steam-shovels stop bucking the ore banks, and produce joyful shrieks on their high-pitched whistles; the Duluth, Mis-sa-be and Northern locomotives, close by, join in a howl of discordant accompaniment; from miners, from gun-toting roughnecks, there comes a harsh pizzicato of revolver shots; and the shouts of the entire assembled population add a bass staff of volume and power to this outlandish frontier music. A little later, on this same day there gathers at Duluth a great crowd of citizens—convinced, at last, by Alfred and Leonidas. They gaze at Car No. 342—new standard ore-car of the D. M. & N.—loaded with ore, and consigned to Lon Merritt. It rumbles into the station carrying all of twenty tons of dark, brownish-purple, soft ore that assays a little better than 65 percent iron—Bessemer. It is worth while noting that a young pine tree is stuck in the middle of the iron ore, and waves, as if to nod a hello to the admiring crowd. There are no longer any laughers at Alfred and Leonidas, who are now, by public acclamation, the iron barons of the North Country. The public feeling is, at last: by God—they've *done* it! Peter Kimberly, the famous furnace man from Sharon, has leased three forties in Town 58-16 from the Merritts' Biwabik Mountain Iron Company. He has contracted to mine at least 300,000 tons per year as a minimum—and is paying the Biwabik Company a royalty of half a dollar for every ton.

But, what's still more important, significant, what takes Lon and Alfred absolutely out of the woods, is the coming of Henry W. Oliver, the plow and shovel man from Pittsburgh. Oliver knows Andy Carnegie, himself; he has been the boyhood pal of Andy's brother Tom, and he knows Henry Clay Frick—intimately. Clean-cut of face, with kind, dark eyes that contradict the rather grim lips hiding behind his gray mustache, Oliver travels to the Vermilion, to Two Harbors, and is not greatly impressed. But then an assay card of a specimen of soft iron, labeled "P-Violet," coming from the Mis-sa-be Mountain Mine, is put before him. That iron has been mined—with a steam-shovel. There are vast telegraphings; presently the brilliant Captain Edward Florada, with sad eyes that look out of a fine, lean face, comes rushing up from Iron Mountain, Michigan. This is the Florada whose widow you would have thought Andy Carnegie might at least have pensioned—because Florada's honest work on the Mis-sa-be has made millions—untold millions—for Andy who said pioneering didn't pay. Florada, guided by John E., sees the amazing layout in the wink of an eye; it is Florada who must have credit for realizing, next after Lon and Alf, the revolution that these still insignificant holes in the ground are going to bring to American steel.

So in 1892 Henry Oliver leased the Mis-sa-be Mountain Mine from the Merritt boys, paid them a bonus of $75,000 in cash—who'd ever seen so much money? Oliver guaranteed to mine a minimum of 400,000 tons of iron per year from their Mis-sa-be Mountain, and he contracted to pay them the corking royalty of sixty-five cents for every ton. The Mis-sa-be Mountain, alone, was now sure of earning better than quarter of a million a year for the Merritts, for K. D. Chase, for the rest of the stockholders. Then there was the Mountain

Iron that they'd work themselves; then there was
the **D. M. & N.**—a little gold-mine, no less, for the
railroad already had made traffic contracts with
Kimberly, with Oliver—to carry their iron to the
Lake at the high rate of eighty cents for every ton
of ore. The railroad, so shrewdly laid out by the
Merritt boys, was stretching its tracks toward Biwabik, toward Hibbing, where new great finds of
ore-basins were making explorers rub their eyes.
The railroad would have a corner on carrying all
the Mis-sa-be ore. Alfred and Leonidas were all
set now; soon they'd be putting their money in—
barrels, that's the word for it—

And yet, was not their work in the revolution, in
the founding of the final magnificence of the American steel industry—if they'd only realized it—finished? They'd found the treasure, invented a marvelously cheap way of robbing the earth of it;
they'd planned and built an excellently convenient
railroad to pour it down to Lake Superior, where
the long, lean-bellied ore-boats waited for it. Their
obscure Promethean part was played; their essential work was done. But they didn't know it. It is
possible to understand why Leonidas, with his vivid
dreams of empire, of a magnificent steel industry
for Duluth itself, insisted, kept charging ahead,
defying the enormous money-power of iron-masters, of capitalists down below. But it is strange

that Alfred, who never seemed to forget the essential fact that he was, after all, only a bushwhacker —didn't prevail on Lon to cash in, to call it a day. Strong hands were already reaching out toward their treasure; extremely business-like poker-faces began to sit across the tables from them. Through their close friend, and attorney, Moses Clapp— later a distinguished United States Senator—Lon and Alf had seen the color of eight millions of dollars, offered them by the Minnesota Iron Company, for their interest in the mines, the railroad. They could have salted that away—and they could then have sat pretty. So, for the rest of their lives, they, and the whole Ne-con-dis, might be sitting on the world, as the saying goes. . . .

Yet they turned down all offers. Lon was like Carlyle's hero, Ram Dass, "with fire enough in his belly to burn up the whole world." Fierce-eyed, supremely confident, bull-necked and looking like a dressed-up blacksmith, Lon planned ore-docks, ordered hundreds of ore-cars, schemed a network of rails over the whole Mis-sa-be Range, and on north, even to Winnipeg. Alfred, bespectacled, droopmustached, the very image of a lumberman imperfectly metamorphosed into a magnate, felt that the fortunes of all minor Merritts, and dozens of other stockholders as well, demanded Merritt hands to distribute this treasure that all America was now needing, wanting. Together these two brothers were incredibly generous, and consequently, simple; they believed that here was enough wealth for everybody; and, though in drinking they confined themselves to fresh milk, tea and coffee, theirs was, at this moment, precisely the spirit of a sailor home on shore-leave after two years before the mast. Not only all of the Merritts, weak or strong, but every one of their friends, less fortunate pioneers, had jobs, for the asking, in the manifold Merritt enterprises. And not only jobs: "I helped my friends *get in on* the properties," said Leonidas, and there's none to gainsay that honest man. "When I found out what it was worth, I indorsed paper, loaned money from our bank." Alfred, though less impulsive, was fully as brotherly; and together these so-different men were, you might say—communistic. A Duluth newspaper of the old days sums up their status in 1892.

"The Merritts were at this time riding the crest of the wave. At a conservative figure their holdings could have been sold for ten million dollars. They had to a remarkable degree the good will of the people of Duluth and St. Louis County. Their credit was exceedingly high, and a note with the name of Merritt on the end or back of it, at a low rate of interest, would command a premium from bankers anywhere."

174

To understand the events which follow, it is necessary to realize that Alfred and Leonidas believed there was enough for everybody—in those cut-throat business days of the 'nineties when men mostly succeeded because they knew there was never enough for one.

VI

Lon and Alf were nothing, were insignificant
specks, were motes of humanity, lost in America's
growing vast turmoil—of rumbling ore trains; of
hundreds of long ore-boats gliding down the Lakes
in sunshine, in fog, snow, rain; of roaring fireworks
of Bessemer converters; of fantastically glowing
chemistry that went on in the new open-hearth furnaces; of the endless white-hot ribbons of molten
steel that poured from the rolling mills in the lush
heart of America at the foot of the Lakes. Who
were Alf and Lon—in those masterful financial
consolidations by means of which Carnegie's partners were forcing the cost of steel-making down,
down, by means of which they were making steel
democratic. It was inevitable that the Mis-sa-be
iron-basins should make a sensation down below in
Pittsburgh—with never a mention of the names of
the obscure bushwhackers who'd found them. It
was natural, fateful, foreordained, that some practical ironmaster, and not Lon—who had never quite
gotten the smell of balsam boughs out of his clothes
—should make the builders of our new iron Amer-

ica aware of these absolutely needful stores of cheap, pure iron.

In the midst of the gravest crisis ever faced by the Carnegie Company, in the bloody industrial war of the summer of 1892, Henry Oliver brought his astounding news from the north, to Henry Frick. "What I've been wanting for my own furnaces, and what all of us have simply got to have," said the dark-eyed plow-maker, "is a cheap, uninterrupted supply of high-grade, Bessemer iron ore." Then the kind-eyed enthusiast told Frick— who was always objective in a most hard-boiled manner—of what the steam-shovels were now beginning to turn up in the new country sixty miles north of Duluth on the Mis-sa-be Range. Lon might have embroidered his story to Frick with details of the glory of the Merritts' pioneer deeds; Oliver simply talked cheap, sure iron.

Frick's light gray eyes—every bit as hard to look into as old Lewis Howell Merritt's eyes had been—lighted up. He forgot his annoyance at the way the striking workmen had just massacred his Pinkerton detectives by the river at Homestead; he leaned forward—

"You see, Mr. Frick," said Oliver, who was a thousand times more economical with words than Leonidas, "I've already formed the Oliver Mining Company. I have a lease on the great Mis-sa-be

177

Mountain mine." Frick's peculiar eyes gleamed, as
Oliver told him of ore cars that could be loaded
with five scoops of a steam-shovel, of grandly simple, open holes in the ground, needing no shafts, no
pumps, no air-compressors, no quickly depreciat-
ing machinery, no annoyingly expensive upkeep.
Oliver simply talked iron ore—that was going to be
mined for less than five cents a ton for labor. When
Lon had tried to describe this to Frick, it had
sounded fantastic, and Frick had cut that honest
man off short, and no wonder. But Henry Oliver
was a manufacturer, was practical.

Oliver told Carnegie's indispensable right-hand
man of that remarkable chain of soft-ore basins at
the foot of the Mis-sa-be hills so handy to Duluth,
to Lake Superior—no matter who'd found them—
but here was the greatest reserve of pure iron ore
ever uncovered in human history! Figures could
not yet accurately describe the indefinite millions
of tons that lay up there—so convenient just under
the gravel; and the railroad to haul the iron down
to the lake was nearly completed—

A few days before this momentous meeting with
Oliver, Frick had been shot, nearly fatally, by the
anarchist, Alexander Berkman; now he forgot the
pain of his hardly mended wounds. And why not—
for here was the chance to push costs down, the
chance that would make all the expense of this

strike, even, look like nothing. Frick, much better than his master, Carnegie, knew the precariousness of the American supply of iron ore, its annoying variations in price, its absolute, its fundamental necessity. Frick had worried over the vanishing American reserves of it; he knew that the specular hematite of the Marquette wouldn't last forever; that the red ore of the Gogebic would one day be scarce; that the iron underground in Alabama wasn't rich; that the reserves in Colorado weren't much—and deucedly costly to haul. And what would be the cost of iron ore they might pretty soon have to import from Cuba, from Chile? Now, here was a practical iron-master across his desk from him, and not some outlandish backwoodsman—like Leonidas—but here was Oliver. Oliver really understood Frick's obsession, knew the American manufacturer's absolute necessity, to make all costs reasonable, and as nearly as possible, negligible! "On what basis can we get together, Mr. Oliver?"

Oliver must have money, to work his new leases, to develop his new Mis-sa-be Mountain mine. Quickly the deal was arranged: Oliver would turn over to the Carnegie Company one-half the stock of the Oliver Mining Company, in return for a loan of a half-million dollars, to be secured by a mortgage on the ore properties. Oliver, it must be remembered, unlike Alfred and Leonidas, had no pride of discovery about these Mis-sa-be ore basins; he was clear-headed and simply wanted sure ore for his own plow-factory. So, in the wink of an eye, Napoleonically, the bargain was as good as closed. Letters, cables, went from Frick to Rannoch in Scotland. But Andrew Carnegie wouldn't hear of such folly. Iron-ore pioneering never had paid. "Oliver's ore bargain just like him—nothing in it," wrote the philanthropist, remote, cool, comfortable, and free from cares in Perthshire, in a letter to Frick dated August 29, 1892.

Frick disobeyed his master's orders, sealed the bargain with Oliver: now he'd never need worry again about iron ore. "After the bargain was made," said Frick to his friend and biographer, Colonel George Harvey, "I was fully convinced that this combination was the most advantageous that ever had been, or ever could be made for the Carnegie Company."

In this quaint manner began the final phenomenal rise of Andrew Carnegie toward domination of American steel. "The story," writes the historian Bridge, "of the way the Carnegie Company acquired its great ore mines on Lake Superior is the story of a huge profit made with hardly a dollar of investment, and the accepting of an impregnable position in the industrial world with a reluctant and complaining consent."

The iron age had now really arrived, thanks entirely to the hope of unlimited ore; at the helm was Henry Clay Frick, coolest and boldest of Vulcans. At Homestead the strikers surrendered; in Pittsburgh the steely-eyed steelmaster ordered and planned, with Gayley, with the genial Charlie Schwab, with Clemson, with W. E. Corey and the rest of that band of materialistically dreaming, iron-smelting, steel-rolling desperadoes, affectionately called "my young geniuses" by their jolly master, Andrew Carnegie. In the rolling-mills, half-naked puddlers sweat, are burned sometimes, but still cheer at their new records for ingots of steel. At Braddock, Munhall, Duquesne, in the many-stacked mills on the shabby banks of those sad and dirty rivers, recruits to the growing army of pulpit-boys gaze in fascination through their goggles, as with cunning levers they control new Bessemer converters, egg-shaped monsters that tremble with the dreadful birth of steel going on inside them, that belch out fountains of violet, then orange, and at last pure white flames. Toward these man-made hells, down the convenient, clear-blue Great Lakes, longer and longer processions of ore-boats glide, their whistles baying, their funnels smoking mightily. Five thousand tons and more of iron ore at a single haul are carried from Lake Superior's rim in the bellies of these strange barges, toward the grimy, the sinister, the absolutely necessary forges by the Allegheny, the Monongahela. Here the red ore from the north meets, crashes and clangs together with the gray coke and white limestone from the eastern mountains—to fuse into pig-iron. Here, purified by fire, the pig-iron changes into the steel that is the frame of the new, fantastic American democracy that slaves—not knowing why—at its job of changing luxuries into necessities, for everybody. For the Ne-con-dis, all this roaring, this pounding, should be like the dreadful, the unearthly kettle-drum music of the Scherzo of the immortal Ninth Symphony—portentous.

But Lon and Alf, way off there at the head of the lakes? Why—they are at the root and bottom of this epical movement; and they know it. They are entirely in tune with their times; with the rest of the Ne-con-dis they are happy, and sure of the future because they know America must have their Mis-sa-be treasure.

VII

Not one moment longer is Lon going to stand big Donald Grant's nonsense. They've got to have ore cars: if the Duluth and Winnipeg hasn't got the money or the push to build them—why—the new Mis-sa-be road'll have to bust with 'em, and build into Duluth, go it alone!

"Look here, Don Grant—you've been abusing me long enough!" Lon jumps from his chair, starts for the huge Grant slowly, with a walk that's curiously light, panther-like, for a man of Lon's forty-eight years, and one hundred and ninety pounds.

Grant is enormous, and powerful, towers over Leonidas and looks as if he could put him in his pocket and walk away with him. Lon walks toward him, swaying a little, with an intolerable gleam in his eyes. "Grant—you talk about annihilating me—"

Grant's friends jump up, some as if to interfere, some looking for an exit. Lon's words are curiously even, his voice is low. "I want to tell you that you are a cur." His voice rises a little, and Grant's forehead is, you might imagine, dampish.

183

"You couldn't lick anybody but a poor crippled boy."

Lon is right under Grant now, boring into the big man's eyes with that unbearable gaze of his.

"Come on! Tackle me!"

Then Lon looks round the room at Grant's friends. And he shouts:

"Come on—I can lick the whole outfit of you!"

He waits—

Grant slumps into a chair. A newspaper report of this momentous business conference, when the fate of the Mis-sa-be road and the Mis-sa-be mines hung balanced, has it that Lon's adversary burst into an incontinent fit of weeping. Nobody in those days of early '93 could stand up to Lon Merritt. He was urged along by the momentum of the terrific success that had suddenly come as a result of thirty years of not acknowledged failure: and this great Merritt enterprise must not stop, must not even hesitate, must go on, now, now. After all, Donald Grant, K. D. Chase and the rest of them were contractors, were bankers, who'd come in afterwards, put their good money in, true enough, but didn't they see the danger of broken traffic contracts, didn't they realize that Peter Kimberly, with his lease of the Biwabik mine, was already threatening to ship his ore out over the Duluth and Iron Range road, that was building in toward him? Lon

184

must have ore-cars! Lon snorted his disgust at this feeble crew of his partners; and he still lived in a world where business battles might be won by fists.

And anyway, the Merritts could get along without Grant and Chase, now that John D. Rockefeller himself—

For a moment, in that ominous winter of '92-'93, it did look as if the Merritts were in a tight place. The Duluth, Mis-sa-be, and Northern road never had had an outlet of its own to the Lake, had linked up, you'll remember, with the Duluth and Winnipeg at Stony Brook on the St. Louis River —and its ore reached the Lake across the Bay, at Superior. The Duluth and Winnipeg had promised to build seven hundred and fifty ore-cars that winter, had flunked out, hadn't built one. The Merritt boys had built 1,500 themselves, in two hectic years, and they'd had to scratch round—as Alf used to say —to do it. But to haul the red ore that would presently be roaring down, from Henry Oliver's diggings at Mis-sa-be Mountain, from Kimberly at Biwabik, from their own great mine at Mountain Iron—1,500 ore-cars were nothing!

They couldn't wait, or rather, they wouldn't wait: such was Lon and Alfred's maniacal eagerness. Why not build right down into Duluth, build their own docks, and cars? All of Duluth was cheering for them, now, at last. St. Louis County had intimated that it might bond itself for a bonus of $250,000 to help them. To the devil with the Duluth and Winnipeg road, and with their prudent, faint-hearted partners. Why—the world was at their feet now. Here was the favorably-known promoter, C. W. Wetmore—a brick of a chap, Alf later called him—who'd come all the way from New York, from Wall Street. Wetmore was simply wild about their Mis-sa-be, had already made promises. And what connections this Wetmore did have! In spite of himself, Leonidas was flattered, and who blames him, when Captain Alec McDougall had introduced him to Wetmore, who was associated in the American Steel Barge Company and, consequently, with John D. Rockefeller himself. Those famous financiers of the Barge Company wanted contracts to carry all of the Mis-sa-be ore down the Lakes in their ore boats; and what if it was going to take a big wad of money to extend the Mis-sa-be road the twenty-six miles from Columbia Junction into Duluth, and to build all their own ore-cars, and ore-docks? Wetmore had already absolutely assured Lon and Alfred of $1,600,000 to finish their road—provided the Barge Company might haul their ore.

Quickly the papers were signed, and on February 3d, K. D. Chase resigned from the presidency of the Duluth, Mis-sa-be, and Northern road; Alfred Merritt—good news!—was elected to succeed him. "Everything is all hunk-a-dori now," said Alf to a newspaper interviewer. The rights and wrongs of the sad break with their old partners are obscure; Lon, indignantly, was sure the Ne-con-dis were about to be frozen out by alleged nefarious dealings between Grant and Chase and the Minnesota Iron Company. And yet—

Yet that honest man, the Honorable and later United States Senator, Moses Clapp, could find no crookedness in Lon and Alfred's adversaries, and the whole matter may be summed up, perhaps, by remembering that Lon and Alfred were furiously impatient while their partners were—prudent. To the *St. Paul Pioneer Press,* Don Grant said:

". . . I do not believe that . . . handing over a controlling interest to the American Steel Barge Company, under the conditions imposed, would be for the best interests of myself or anybody else. . . . I marvel that the innocent lambs, led to the slaughter, lick the hand that is raised to annihilate them."

But preposterous! Imagine anybody calling the self-reliant Lon and the shrewd Alf—innocent lambs. . . .

Terrific events were in the making in the north country now, and Alfred and Leonidas were, at last, in really fast financial company. "The *Tribune's* announcement," reported the Pittsburgh *Gazette* for February 7th, 1893, "that John D. Rockefeller has brought about the consolidation of the American Steel Barge Company and the West Superior Rolling Mills, thereby forming a corporation commanding $7,000,000 capital, created a sensation among mining men in the Lake Superior District. . . . That Rockefeller is reaching out for the vast iron production of the Mis-sa-be Range is evident to all persons conversant with this field, which in two years has been developed into the greatest iron-producing country in the world."

Leonidas was exuberant. Newsgatherers, investors, capitalists, in these thumping days, flocked round him. "The Merritt syndicate," he told them, "has complete control of the D. M. & N. . . . They own and control it for all time, and the Rockefellers and the Barge Company behind them will furnish all the money that may be needed." Such was Wetmore's promise; Lon and Alfred, woodsmen, believed in promises. They had, among the men with whom they'd lived, almost always had excellent reason to. And it looked as if Wetmore was certainly delivering the goods!

Because Lon rushed to Chicago—this was getting to be big business!—in response to urgent telegrams from Wall Street. He was met by Mr.

Wetmore, and Mr. Rockefeller's attorney, Murray, and was handed a draft for $350,000. "Which I shoved in my vest pocket," testified Leonidas, "the same as a southern gentleman would a roll of bills. . . . In fact, I remember their reprimanding me by saying this was a large amount of money and I ought to take care of it."

In Duluth, Alfred, who now often wore a white collar, did not wait for ratification by the stockholders, but let the contracts for the Mis-sa-be railroad extensions, and for the ore-docks, in his own name. It was, maybe, not entirely prudent of him, still—

Leonidas was back from Chicago, and announced: "The Mis-sa-be road has now in its treasury $400,000, and not a dollar of debt. The company expects to cover the entire Mis-sa-be Range with its tracks and spurs, and extensions will begin as soon as frost is out of the ground."

This was, indeed, the time of the apotheosis of the Merritt Ne-con-dis. Alf and Lon were called multi-millionaires by everybody. Young John E., up on the range, was pointed out by seasoned explorers, with awe: he was known to have a standing offer of $1,000,000 for his Mountain Iron stock but he only laughed at it. Even the gentle woodsman, Cassius, and the youngest of all the Merritt brothers, Andrus, to their surprise became magnates;

and the whole Ne-con-dis buzzed at their multifarious jobs with a frenetic energy, like the super-Americans that most of them were. The last little wrinkled ledges of ice tinkled into the northern rivers; sap turned the maple trunks a shiny black; the tender red-yellow flames of the willow tips changed to a bright yellow green—and great men arrived in Duluth to be shown over the Mis-sa-be Range in Lon and Alfred's handsome railroad car. The Reverend Mr. Fred T. Gates arrived, enthusiastic, cordial, with finely modeled features, abundant, wavy hair, and a rare gift of eloquence. For eight years he had been the distinguished pastor of the Central Baptist Church of Minneapolis, only to be called to higher spheres of usefulness, for he was now in charge of the benevolences of John D. Rockefeller, and was famous, justly, for being with Goodspeed the founder of the University of Chicago.* The Reverend Mr. Gates met Leonidas, and their respect was instant and mutual. In his own way Gates was a pioneer, though he'd probably never worn shoe-pacs, nor had his forehead chafed at the cruel rub of a misery-strap. Just the same, this man of God was among the very first of the great organizers of philanthropy, and had the insight to see the good that lay dormant in the new, immense American fortunes. He possibly would

* See Appendix F, page 225.

have had a rather uncomfortable time in a birch-bark boat in white water, yet he harbored sincere and splendid dreams, of bonds turning into immense eleemosynary foundations and life-saving laboratories. In Mr. Rockefeller's own words, the Reverend Mr. Gates had "a passion for accomplishing great and far-reaching benefits for mankind." Finally—and this too is Mr. Rockefeller's appreciation—the Reverend Mr. Gates believed, along with the philanthropist, "that we could never have too many good mines." And why not? Because, for this dreamer, more mines must mean more organized mercy, more millions for mending mankind's misery.

The great almoner saw the steam-shovels bucking the ore-banks in the immense new open-pit mines of the Mis-sa-be, was impressed, and who would not have been? Mr. Rockefeller had hardly made a mistake in buying his first $400,000 worth of Mis-sa-be bonds from the enthusiastic Wetmore.

Never in the adventurous annals of the Ne-con-dis had there been such a hopeful spring, and Lon and Alfred only laughed at rumors, disturbing to faint hearts, of tight money in Wall Street, of "the United States Treasury scraping on bare bottom" as some folks were saying. It's true that there had been trouble, down below, with the first shipments of their Mis-sa-be ore, which was so powdery, so fine, that it clogged the furnaces, even blew some of them up. But never fear, there was the indomitable Henry Oliver, there was Frick, who knew there *must* be some way to smelt this iron that was going to be so cheap, that was so utterly limitless. For the Carnegie engineers, living in the tradition of Holley and the famous Bill Jones, nothing was impossible, and they were already building furnaces of a new design; were finding the Mis-sa-be ore was all right if you mixed it with the rockier ore from upper Michigan. . . . Everything was, after all, hunk-a-dori. Enormous new ore-basins were being discovered on the Range to the west, at Hibbing, and their Mis-sa-be road would have the hauling of all of it—down the easy grade, at eighty cents for every ton. This was the first spring that Leonidas had no time to hear the cheerful "kong-que-ree-e-e!" of the red-winged blackbirds. In his front yard at Oneota, Alfred saw robins, but didn't have to be cheered up by their "cheerily—cheerily—cheerup!"

VIII

God—it had been a tough pull, this summer, certainly tougher'n any portage he'd ever packed over. This big business was ticklish—you had to watch yourself sharper than in any white water you might get sucked into, in your birch-bark boat. Dickering with these big fellows in New York wasn't simple —like putting Don Grant in his place. You could always see Grant, or anybody else at the Head of the Lakes, but here you sat in reception rooms— high-toned ones—and waited, and looked at doors, always doors, doors marked "PRIVATE," and when they said private, they meant it. Leonidas wiped his forehead; funny—up at Duluth it never did get so close, so clammy hot. He dated his letter August 30, 1893; he had just sat himself down to write certain great news to his daughter, Ruth.

"My dear Ruth," wrote Leonidas, "I have been so anxious to see you that I scarcely know what to do. . . ."

Lon stopped to think: why—he'd left Duluth in May, to be in New York just a few days, to find out why that fellow Wetmore wasn't keeping his

promises, wasn't coming through with that more
than a million dollars he was going to raise for the
Mis-sa-be railroad. And here it was August, without a sight of his good wife, or Ruth, or his boys
Lucien and Harry.

"I do not worry about any of you because I know
you are all good and will do right about everything," wrote Lon. . . .

Wetmore had certainly fallen down after that
first $400,000 worth of bonds he'd sold to Mr.
Rockefeller. Here Lon had landed, in streets
walled in by tall buildings, much more confusing,
more mysterious than the Mis-sa-be bush had been
to him, even in the earliest days. Leonidas didn't
know what he would have done—without the Reverend Mr. Gates. It was Gates who'd got him the
money, that Alf, Cashie, John E., all the Merritt
boys up on the Range were simply yelling for—and
who blamed them? The workmen weren't getting
paid; the creditors were beginning to get ugly—
even though this was the famous Merritt credit.
. . . But just when things looked like receiverships,
like worse, Mr. Gates would smooth things over,
would save the situation with a draft for real money.
Of course, it was true that these were loans, that
Lon had had to put up his mine stocks, his railroad
stocks with Mr. Rockefeller. But times were hard

for everybody, money was tight—and the work *must* go on.

Leonidas sighed, and wiped his forehead again. Everything was hunk-a-dori now. "I am quite content since yesterday," he wrote. Ah, Ruth—there was a real Merritt woman! How proud she'd be! "I am elected now President of a great corporation, perhaps the greatest in the world. . . ."

But what a tight squeak it had been. Wetmore had got himself into a terrible mess trying to raise that money; Lon had saved him, by indorsements, by putting up mine stock for him—good thing the Merritts owned so much of the Mis-sa-be Range. . . . But the Reverend Mr. Gates had come to the rescue, in June. . . . That was a worried month, when the toughs up on the Range were actually getting ready to mob the Merritts! But just at the worst moment, Gates had actually gotten Lon an audience with John D. Rockefeller himself, who, as Gates now remembered it, had talked mainly about the weather, at Duluth and elsewhere. But Lon distinctly seemed to recall that the philanthropist, who seemed a genuinely kindly man, in spite of his tight-drawn mouth, had said, that if it could be arranged for a consolidation he would be proud to become Lon's partner and backer. Mr. Rockefeller had wanted to put in some of his own properties along with the immense Mis-sa-be holdings of the Merritt boys—"get our eggs in one basket and take care of it," he'd said.

Anyway—even if Mr. Rockefeller had not said that, but had had Lon in simply to talk to him about the weather,* nothing else, still the fact remained that the great consolidation was made. "I can hear," wrote Lon to his dark-haired daughter Ruth, "above the roar of the carts on the stone pavement, the bellowing of the bulls and the growls of the bears on the exchange. To my right we have the U.S. Sub-Treasury where silver and gold are piled up like piles of stone. . . ."

Well—now that Leonidas himself was President of the Lake Superior Consolidated Iron Mines, and the Merritt family had the majority of the Directors, the majority of the stock, they'd surely have piles of gold, too, in exchange for all their Mis-sa-be iron. Mr. Rockefeller had put in his Spanish-American mine, in Cuba, and his Gogebic mines in Michigan. It's true he'd not taken any stock in the new Consolidation—just bonds. And those bonds were a first mortgage on the whole immense property, but—

"I have a very interesting boy who tends the office," Lon's pen scratched over the paper. "He is gentle and good, and makes me think of Harry and Lucien. Of course he thinks I am about the best man in the world. Every day he orders lunch to my

* See Appendix G, page 226.

room and we set down and eat it together. Today we had fried chicken, bread, tea, potatoes, peaches and cream. . . ."

Maybe it would have been better for Alfred to have come down to New York in the first place. Alf was shrewd. . . . Alf and Andrus had hurried to New York just a few days ago—protesting the big deal wasn't right, saying Mr. Rockefeller ought to take stock too. But the Reverend Mr. Gates had set them right, had explained that Mr. Rockefeller, as a prudent financier, was past speculation. And Gates had surely been fair, let them put their own valuation on the Mis-sa-be mines, the Mis-sa-be railroad. He wouldn't think of letting Alf, as he had a chance to do, sell the Rathbun mine for $500,000 cash—to pay the Merritt debts, no. And now Alf, Leonidas, the rest of them owned between ten and twenty millions of dollars worth of Consolidated stock—

"Tell Harry," wrote Lon to Ruth, "if he was here he could get Bananas galore and peaches and pears great basketsful for ever so little money. . . ."

Money! That was the deuce of it. Money was so confoundedly tight now. Why, Mr. Rockefeller had had to pledge his own personal securities, that nasty day when he'd had to send gold to Duluth, by express, to stop the riots, to keep the workmen and their families from starving. Why, even the

Merritt boys back there—with all their wealth in those Mis-sa-be basins—could hardly pay their grocery bills, had hardly enough to eat. . . . This panic—

But everything was all right now. "I am going in a few minutes down to Long Island Sound, to take a sail on a crack (boat), it is the first day I had any time to do anything of the kind this summer." And he signed his letter, "Good-by, Lon Merritt."

There was only one thing that bothered Lon, just a wee bit, as he closed his desk. His own stock, Alfred's, a lot of the other boys' stock in the new company, was up for collateral with Mr. Rockefeller—backing loans Wetmore had made, they themselves had to make, to keep work going on the mines, on the railroad. Those notes, were they demand notes, or were they time? Lon wasn't quite sure. . . . But Mr. Gates would take care of that. Lon straightened up, put on his black, broad-brimmed western hat. Oliver's, Kimberly's immense tonnage was beginning to roll out of the Mis-sa-be Mountain and Biwabik—paying big royalties, paying eighty cents a ton down their railroad. After all, the Merritt boys had discovered this Mis-sa-be Range, developed it, really owned the best part of it; those debts would be wiped out—less than no time. Everything would be hunk-a-dori now.

IX

"I was to blame—" says Leonidas, and he bows his head, then straightens up and faces them all once more.

Eighteen years have passed; it is November 22nd of 1911; Lon sits—an unknown Northwesterner—telling his story to a roomful of notables, in an austere room, at Washington. Long ago, as far back as 1895, the Mis-sa-be Iron Range—that was once Lon and Alf's Mis-sa-be—passed all other American ranges in annual production of iron. This year of 1911 as Lon sits at the long table, bombarded by questions from distinguished Congressmen, the basins at the foot of the low Grandmother Hills of Mis-sa-be Wasju are giving up more iron than all of the other iron mines in America put together.

Lon's hair is graying now, but his beetling eyebrows are still pitch-black, and from under them gaze those same eyes with their old dark defiant flame. He's not beaten, mind you—he remembers that he and Alfred and the Merritt boys found the Mis-sa-be, and that he was—in '93—the President

199

of the Lake Superior Consolidated Iron Mines, in that hectic panic year when the freighters from Duluth took their first six hundred thousand tons of red ore down Kitchi Gammi. . . . But a year ago, in 1910, mining sixty percent of America's ore, his Mis-sa-be has shipped close to thirty millions of tons.

There are moments, as Lon talks in this long Washington room, when you can hear a pin drop, when hard-boiled Washington correspondents lean forward as interested as children listening to their grandpa, when they get red in the face, and swallow a little. Around Lon's eyes there are much deeper wrinkles now, partly cynical, for he's no longer as good a Methodist as his mother Hepzibeth had taught him to be. But mainly these creases are explorer's wrinkles, for he has kept going back to the bush, and it's only a little while back—though now near seventy—that he was hunting for iron. To look at him, you'd never suspect he had been one of the prime causes of the phenomenal rise, between '96 and 1900, of the profits of the Carnegie Steel Company from eight millions a year to forty millions. Yet Colonel George Harvey has truly written that "Chief among the contributions to this amazing result was the acquisition of mines capable of yielding huge quantities of Bessemer ore." Those

"THEN THERE WAS THE MOUNTAIN IRON THAT THEY'D WORK THEMSELVES"

"LON'S HAIR IS GRAYING NOW, BUT HIS BEETLING EYEBROWS
ARE STILL PITCH-BLACK"

were the Mis-sa-be mines that Lon and Alf discovered.

Lon's recital is clear, is strong, has a real touch
of the Homeric about it, as he tells his strained,
attentively silent audience of the thirty years of
Merritt adventure that preceded their immense
discovery. But, alas, when certain Congressmen,
who plainly despise him, and certain very learned
lawyers, get to posing him questions about business,
tangle him up with talk about demand notes, col-
laterals, contracts—Leonidas is amazingly ignorant. He hesitates then; his voice even breaks a
little; plainly, when it comes to big business, Lon
must be a sap—as the saying goes. It is grotesque
to think that this is the man whose primitive grub-
bings had helped to get the heirs of Henry Oliver
the seventeen millions of dollars for which they
turned in their little one-sixth interest in the Oliver
Mining Company to the new United States Steel
Corporation. Henry Oliver and Lon in some ways
were much alike—and were always good friends.

Leonidas is so distressingly ignorant about the
terrific business transactions of those panic years
of '93 and '94, that it is fair to ask why influential
men would have allowed him any part in business
at all. Today, Congressman Gardner, one of the
most insistent of his inquisitors, asks him has he no

papers to show what defended his rights to the mines, to the railroad, in the first instance—and has he no copy of the contract under which he put up those large bunches of security? Lon only bows his head, and answers: "No—" Yet, look at him as he sits among all these notables: as a man he is by no means the least of them. Why is he a poor man now? The prosperity of dozens of lesser folk who held on—during those parlous times—to their Missa-be stock, is well known. Surely you remember the immortal cook of the Biwabik, Mr. Housell, whom John E. paid half of his forty-dollar-a-month wages in stock of the Biwabik. Housell sold out his little holdings to the new United States Steel Corporation for $95,000—and bought a nice ranch in Colorado—

About Lon's story there's something incredible —yet you see with half an eye that he's nothing if not a simple, square-shooting backwoodsman. At one moment, torn by memories that shall here be nameless, he nearly breaks down, asks to be excused for a minute. At another, when his anger breaks into a flame, you can understand how his sarcasm, his talent for vituperation, have made him all his trouble, made him almost unfit to associate with reasonable capitalists, business men. Once, when he's justifiably attacked for his utter lack of business ability by a famous lawyer—who maybe snarls just a bit too much—Congressman Stanley, Chairman of the solemn Congressional Committee, comes to Lon's defense. "I went to the State of Minnesota," says Stanley, red in the face, "I went to the City of Duluth, went up on the Range, went among the lumbermen with whom they"—the Merritts—"had explored in the snow, and found that not one man, but the people of Minnesota, regarded these men, in a way, as we regard Boone in Kentucky, and as they regard Houston in Texas, with gratitude, with reverence."

Lon's memory of his lamentable business entanglements is so bad, that you'd think, at some moments, he is one of those shrewd witnesses who forget—intentionally. Brilliant lawyers scribble questions, which they pass to Chairman Stanley: "When the Merritt brothers, some of them, sold their Consolidated stock to Rockefeller in January, 1894, what did it bring?" Lon bows his head, doesn't even know! Wasn't it all of $900,000? Lon doesn't remember. Hadn't Mr. Rockefeller given the Merritts a chance to buy back more than half of this stock in twelve months—paying him only a fair six percent interest? But Leonidas was confused, and could only explain: "For a long time I've cultivated a forgetter, for reasons of my own." Yet, this is the man who—along with Alf—discovered an iron range containing ore properties, whose value, as Charles Schwab had already testified, might be reasonably estimated at three hundred and thirty-three millions of dollars; who dug, from under the pine needles and gravel, those iron basins that were the pivot, the fulcrum of the gigantic financial goings-on of 1901. For Harvey, the official biographer of Henry Clay Frick, has told: "But for the acquirement of the Mis-sa-be Mines the colossal United States Steel Corporation could not have been organized."

You listen to Lon, here in this long room at this long table at Washington, as his thoughts fumble painfully among arguments about time notes, call loans, and, as an American in today's prosperous America, you thank your stars that the Mis-sa-be Railroad and a large part of the Mis-sa-be ore basins did pass into the strong, the integrating hands of a financier like Mr. Rockefeller. That organizing genius had the ore properties finely in hand, running smoothly, when the time came in 1901 to turn them in to the United States Steel Corporation for sixty-eight million dollars—a price that was low as events have proved, that unquestionably cheated Mr. Rockefeller badly. "Without those mines," said Mr. Rockefeller, slowly, according to Colonel George Harvey, "the United States Steel Corporation could not have survived the stress of its formative period."

Leonidas certainly must have had quaint financial ideas, in those panic days of the winter of '93-'94. "I had no money even to go home," said he, in answer to a question of Congressman Stanley. The audience sat, as Lon said that, in amazement. "I could not conceive," Lon went on, "that I could have gone down with millions, absolute millions of my own and my brothers' money. I could not conceive how in hell, within those few months, without ever spending a cent above my board bill, I could have gone to New York, and lost all those millions."

But surely the whole transaction had been aboveboard; the distinguished attorneys, Rush Taggart and Judge Dillon, had advised Lon, when at last he called them to help him, to sell out to Mr. Rockefeller. "The things that happened at that time are not clear to me. The idea of going down there and losing all this money, not only my money, but my brothers' money, leaving their families stripped, so that they did not even have money to pay streetcar fares, struck me down physically, and, I am sorry to say, for a while mentally," said Leonidas.

"To me," wrote the Reverend Mr. Gates, "Messrs. Dillon and Taggart had nothing but praise for the good faith in which Mr. Rockefeller acted."

"And then you went back into the woods?" asked Congressman Stanley, of Leonidas.

"Yes, sir, after one thing and another, I went back into the woods, in the snow and the cold, and tried to forget all these things. My brother"—that was the explorer, Cashie—"had more nerve than I had. It killed him."

"And you blame yourself for your brother's death, and for all that happened?" asked Stanley, kindly.

Lon's head bowed. "I blame myself for my brother's death, and I blame myself for all their misfortunes. I was to blame."

X

THAT was the manly thing about Leonidas Merritt: that he blamed himself for everything. And
it is amazing that during those black days, just
after Lon got back from New York, that Alfred,
the shrewd one, didn't turn on his brother Leonidas.
But it is one of the comforting things, the happy
parts of the end of this story: that these two,
though so different, remained steadfast, remained
Ne-con-dis, after the tradition of the vanishing
Ojibways who taught them their first lessons in
woodcraft and life.

Alfred, Cashie, John E., Wilbur the giant explorer, young Alvie, Bert—all of them stuck together, were kind to poor Lon, and to each other.
As John D. Rockefeller, himself, has put it: "Probably the most generous people in the world are
the very poor, who assume each other's burdens
in the crises which come so often to the hard-
pressed." These seven among the iron men of the
House of Merritt shared everything, with each
other, with their families. It is a comfort that only

207

one of the brothers left them and went, a rich man, to live in California.

Of course for a while they were blindly furious at their disaster, and Alfred was guilty of an indiscretion, even going so far as to sue Mr. John D. Rockefeller for fraud and misrepresentation it was alleged he had committed when he put his Gogebic mines into the basket with the Merritts' great basins of the Mis-sa-be. . . . In that lawsuit, tried before a jury of twelve good men and true in the United States Circuit Court in 1895, at Duluth, Alfred was actually awarded a verdict of $940,000. The case was, of course, appealed by the defendant, and in the United States Circuit Court of Appeals, sitting at St. Louis, the verdict was reversed by three distinguished judges, and the case sent back for re-trial. But Alf couldn't try it again; hadn't—as he liked to say—a soo-markee. In the first trial he'd had to walk to the courthouse, not being able to afford the nickel for carfare.

In fairness to everybody, it must be stated that, two years later, twenty-one men and women of the Merritt family signed a retraction of their charges of fraud, absolutely clearing the name of Mr. Rockefeller. "It is hereby declared that from recent independent investigations made by us or under our direction we have become satisfied that no misrepresentation was made nor fraud committed by

Mr. Rockefeller, or by his agents or attorneys for him. . . ." Alf, Leonidas, and all their dear ones signed this, which proves that Alf should never have begun his lawsuit at all!

In consideration of their signing this document, the Merritt family were paid a little more than $500,000 by Mr. Rockefeller—and most of this was used to pay part of the debts that still hung over them. To refute Lon's *miserere,* of that day at Washington, 1911, this retraction was very properly brought forward; and, when the Reverend Mr. Gates and Mr. Rockefeller were invited by the committee to present their side of the story in person, they rightly declined. They were justified in pointing to that piece of paper as settling the controversy forever. In his well-reasoned document, entitled "Inside Story of Rockefeller and Missa-be Mines," the Reverend Mr. Gates points out:

"We knew, of course, that it might be charged that the retraction had been purchased with the price of the settlement, but we reflected that honest men making true charges of fraud are not accustomed to retract those charges for a price in money put into their hands."

All that Lon could say, that sad day at Washington, under oath in the long room before Congressmen, news-gatherers, notables, lawyers, was: "If I signed that, Mr. Chairman, knowingly, it

would have been because I wanted to relieve my
family from their destitution and absolute pov-
erty."

And yet, is not the logic on the side of the
Reverend Mr. Gates? * The whole sad business may
be summed up in the words of the conservative
economist, Charles Neil Thomas: "In times of
financial stringency many properties inevitably
change hands."

But time heals everything. The years pass, and
Lon and Alf are comforted—by the new homes
that cover the side of the great gabbro hill back
of prosperous Duluth, by the lights that twinkle
happily from that hillside in the evenings, by the
strings of lights that gleam between the mast-heads
of the processions of red-bellied ore-boats, as, with
deep roars of their whistles, they start down Kitchi
Gammi, to give iron to America. After all, they've
done their bit to start all this. They shouldn't have
been so annoyed, it's true, at losing their fortunes.
But then again, who blames them—for, after all,
for a while it had been their country, this Mis-sa-be
back there, with its moose to shoot when they were
near to starving, with its rapids to near get
drowned in, with its bush, in which they'd one time
near got burned to death.

In reality they were rich—spiritually. For years
after their disaster, they could still sit at the feet

* See Appendix G, page 226.

of the now ancient but still philosophical Hepzibeth, who still sat at her knitting, who in spite of
her near ninety years was a mighty chipper old
lady, who encouraged them to pull on their shoe-
pacs once more, and to hunt, again—for iron.

Alfred had a theory that the Mis-sa-be Range
might extend northeast, all the way through Canada, northeast across unsurveyed country to the
barren land of little sticks, in Labrador; though he
failed to prove it, you'd find him up north there,
rooting around, even in his old age. Alf still liked
to sail the dangerous water of Lake Superior, and,
with his daredevil son, Clark, you'd see him setting
off, now and again, from his shack on Isle Royale
to take a gamble with the storm gods that brood
over that gray sheet of water. Alf would look at his
compass, on a little plank placed across the gun-
wales, and away they'd go, across forty-five miles of
open water, in a little skiff powered by an uncertain
gasoline motor, for a call, in Michigan, on a friend
of the old days.

Lon and John E. looked for iron on the north
shore of Lake Superior. Though not rich, they were
able to hire two Indians, Joe Salt and Joe Pepper.
One nasty November day they were near drowned
crossing South Bay of Lake Nipigon, and to cele-
brate, to commemorate this tight squeak, Leonidas *
wrote a poem for his fellow poet, and nephew:

* See Appendix H, page 227.

"We worked, Johnny boy, on our knees in the waist,
Till we felt in our mouths the coppery taste;
We worked, Johnny boy, for the opposite shore,
Till our sinews and nerves were knotted and sore."

It's true they didn't find merchantable iron, but what helped them out was that they were always trying. Optimists born, visionaries they remained to the last, and they never could seem to realize that, in the words of the sympathetic historian, Van Brunt: "The chance to discover a range like the Mis-sa-be does not come often."

To the very last Lon's face—battered as some old prize-fighter's face would be—looked young. "He was always looking forward," said his nephew Bert. He served Duluth, till he was eighty years old, as Commissioner of Public Utilities, and of Finance, which is strange when you remember what a weird businessman he was in those panic days of the nineties. . . . He lived to the last, stubbornly, in a little house at Oneota, which had become grimy what with the ore-docks, the Mis-sa-be railroad, the great steel industry close by. In this low house, under willows and among lilacs, in rooms whose paper had maybe peeled a little, whose plaster wasn't all that it should be, he tended to his affairs, remained hopeful, sarcastic, defiant, and generous—as always. "All evening he might hardly say a word—

but it was great just to sit there by him," said Bert, the younger brother of Wilbur.

Lon died on May 9th, 1926, in that faintly ramshackle cottage, in this month when the red-winged blackbirds begin to whistle, and when the robins are at the height of their singing. Over his grave there sounded the shots due an old soldier; as his body was lowered, a veteran blew taps. He was buried high on that gabbro hill, above Oneota; his grave looks northeast up the misty, mysterious reaches of Kitchi Gammi; the earth of his grave trembles a little at the rumble of the red-ore trains that roll, day and night, over the tracks of his old Duluth, Mis-sa-be, and Northern—toward those ore-docks that he and Alf had dreamed, and begun to build. The city of Duluth went into official mourning for him for four whole days. He had no debts. He left no will. His fortune was stated, by Ruth, Harry, and Lucien, to consist of $1,500 worth of household goods, $800 miscellaneous, and $150 in cash.

The graves of Alfred and Cassius lie near him, and at the head of all three there are moderate-priced, respectable monuments. But if you wish to see the real markers of these three men of the Ne-con-dis, you must travel to the north; there are fine concrete roads leading to, and all over the Mis-sa-be, now. You may ride, through prosperous little cities with surprising million-dollar high-schools, for miles past strange chains of yawning holes, fantastic chasms they are—miles long, a mile across, and five hundred feet in depth. These pits are the Merritts' inverted monuments—with no name of Merritt on them. Out of these holes has gone the iron they worked so long to discover, that is at the bottom of our cloud-scraping commercial temples, of our millions of motors of the steel age that is America's present glory. As monuments, you'll agree that these holes are inverted, but that is as it should be, as part of the topsy-turviness of life itself.

For who, if not the Merritts, should have been rewarded, materially, for this treasure they found? But then, you are right, many other good men have had their part in it, and the Merritts are not even the first heroes of this story. There are those insignificant bugs, those *Gallionella*—they are living beings too. Down in the holes you'll still find these iron-shrouded microbes, busy at their job of making iron, without thought of reward. So it had to be too, maybe, with these men who were in their small way Prometheans, who after all, though, only found the iron.

Best of all monuments is the Merritt seed that survives, and it should be a comfort to everybody

214

"MAYBE SO," SAID ALF, "BUT I WOULD LIKE TO HAVE TRIED IT—JUST ONCE"

LEONIDAS AT EIGHTY-TWO. "HE WAS ALWAYS LOOKING FORWARD,"
SAID BERT

that in our American land there are plenty of grandchildren, and great-grandchildren, of Lewis Merritt—the man of extremes—and his good wife, Hepzibeth. John E.—honored as the founder of the coöperative creamery at Aitkin, Minnesota, has two rapscallion, red-faced youngsters that are going to make their mark some day. Alf's son, Glen, won the Croix de Guerre, and a Divisional Citation in France, and came back a private, and was honorably discharged. Alf's boy Clark has been a daredevil aviator, a lucky flier he calls himself, and he's still alive. There are Lon's sons, Harry and Lucien, who've dredged the Mississippi and helped deepen harbors along our Atlantic seaboard. Lon has a grandson who—a geologist of all things!—is hunting minerals in Africa. Wilbur has husky sons who are farmers in Montana. Nameless —when it comes to fame—as the *Gallionella* themselves, all these toil like sailors and sea-captains, necessarily, anonymously.

What would have happened to these useful citizens if Lon and Alfred had gotten enormously rich, gotten to be iron barons to rival Jim Hill himself? There are visions, maybe wrong, of welleducated young bundles of futility—permanently decorative in roadsters and raccoon coats.

"Maybe so, maybe so," said Alf Merritt, not long before they took him for his last ride up the gabbro hill, when some one pointed out for his consolation how positively ruinous wealth would have been to the Merritt children.

"Maybe so," said Alf, and his eyes twinkled. "But I would have liked to have tried it—just once."

END OF
SEVEN IRON MEN

EXPLANATORY NOTES

THESE need not be read by those who have been interested in "Seven Iron Men" purely as a story, yarn, or divertisement. Those whose curiosity and feelings have been aroused beyond these limits may find the matter presented in these Appendices of some interest, and valuable to start them on the trail of further investigation.

Appendix A: to Part One

So far as this writer can discover, Professor William Herbert Hobbs, of the University of Michigan, is the first to give George R. Stuntz priority for his observations bearing on the tilting of the Lake Superior Region. In his monograph entitled "The Late Glacial and Post Glacial Uplift of the Michigan Basin," the Professor remarks:

"It is worthy of note that the earliest recognition of the late uplift of the lake region was by a land surveyor of Wisconsin, Mr. G. K. Stuntz" (the Professor means G. R. Stuntz) "who made observations about Lake Superior in the years 1852 and 1853 and published a brief paper in 1870. Stuntz had noticed that on the north shore of Lake Superior there were evidences that the land had recently risen, while on the south side there were signs of recent overflow. Thus in the St. Mary's River, the outlet of Lake Superior, he found a mill race entirely dry, while

217

in the neighborhood a small stream ran into the lake with a swift current. On the southern shore of the lake and particularly toward the west, a flooding of the river mouths was generally observable. This was specially noticeable in the St. Louis River which enters Lake Superior at Duluth."

Professor Hobbs then quotes from Stuntz's paper, which was published in the Proceedings of the American Association for the Advancement of Science, Vol. XVIII, 1870, pp. 206-7, as follows:

"In several parts submerged stumps several feet below the present water level, are found. The numerous inlets surrounding the main bay, when we consider the nature of the soil, and the formation (a tough, red clay), in all of which the water is deep, could not have been excavated in the natural course of events with the water at its present level. The testimony of the Indians also goes to strengthen the same conclusion. At the time of running the State line above mentioned" (this was the Minnesota-Wisconsin boundary), "the Indians, ever jealous of their rights, called me to a council to inquire why I ran the line through Indian land. In the explanation, I gave, using the language of the law, as a starting point, the lowest rapid in the St. Louis River. The chief immediately replied that formerly there was a rapid nearly opposite the Indian village. Start, said he, from that place, and you will be near the treaty line. After he had been further questioned, I learned that it was only a few years since the river was quite rapid at the Indian village. At the time the said line was run the rapid was about one mile by the stream above the village. From these facts I conclude that a change is taking place gradually in the level of this great valley."

SEVEN IRON MEN

Appendix B: to Part One

Stuntz's original observations on artifacts left by presumably prehistoric Americans are embodied in two short papers, read on December 2, 1884, and January 6, 1885, before the Minnesota Academy of Natural Sciences. The first of these reports concerns itself with evidences of early man in Northeast Minnesota; the second is devoted more specifically to mound-builders. In these the genial explorer presents evidence to show how some prehistoric folk, by cunning if crude engineering, damned the Gichi Gummi Sibi (St. Louis) and other rivers, to produce stretches of slack water that would reduce the number of portages, and in general make their water traffic less onerous. He describes rock dams on the Embarrass River above Esquagamo Lake, in the construction of which engineering methods were used that are unknown to the modern Chippewa or Sioux. He calculates, from the depth of peat in the swamp of an old lake so old it is now filled up, that these operations may have taken place 7,200 years (!) ago—assuming that the deposition of peat is at the rate of one inch per 100 years.

North of the Mesabi hills, in what the explorer Nicollet called "The Land of Rocks and Water," Stuntz observed what he took to be plantations of oak, lindens, elms and plum trees. He speculates on what induced these ancient people to occupy such a desolate region, and concludes that they did not come up there as summer-resorters or sportsmen, purely. On the other hand, he was able to detect what seemed to him to be very ancient excavations, made in solid jasper, dump piles, gravel walks from the rock-cut to the dumps, and fragments of charcoal and ashes. Stuntz laboriously traced the water routes of his supposed ancient people along the very rivers and lakes that he, and also Leonidas and his iron men, used in their conquest of the Mis-sa-be. He followed these marvel-

219

ously engineered traffic lanes across the white water called
by the Chippewas "Mukwa-manito-ka-ka-bi-ke," or "Black
Spirit" rapid. Near Vermilion Lake he found evidences of
ancient pottery, and of mining which he takes to have been
done for the purpose of obtaining red ocher. He believes
the aborigines worked their mines by heating the rocks,
dashing water on them, and then pounding them with stone
hammers.

Stuntz's conclusions have been objected to by at least
one later investigator, who claims that the undoubted
dams along these water courses were the work of God (or
Nature)—not of men. It is this writer's opinion that the
old explorer's observations have not been successfully re-
futed. At the same time the question remains in that un-
happy state commmon to all geological and archeological
controversies—unsettled, and impossible to settle. Because, to use that wonderfully pregnant aphorism so beloved by Jacques Loeb, "one cannot experiment with the
past."

Appendix C: to Part Two

For the admittedly sketchy and inadequate geological
background of this story, I wish here to acknowledge my
indebtedness to the magnificent geological history of the
Lake Superior Region to be found in Monograph LII,
of the United States Geological Survey, by the late
Professor Charles Richard Van Hise, and Professor
Charles Kenneth Leith. The reader who might perhaps be
inspired to pursue these awe-inspiring and impersonal
matters further, would do well to consult, also, Monograph XLIII, United States Geological Survey, entitled
"The Mesabi Iron-bearing District of Minnesota," by
Charles Kenneth Leith. Chapter VII of that work sums up,
in a masterpiece of prose writing, the fantastic supposed
history of that rock-ribbed and desolate region, from
those misty and entirely unattainable days when the

ancient Mesabi hills first—presumably—began to lift up their heads. For the study of the outlandish conjectural history of the Great Lakes, I recommend that the reader consult Monograph LIII, of the same series, by the rock-readers, Frank Leverett and Frank B. Taylor. It is to their detailed presentation of these matters that I am indebted for the small sketch outlined on pages 37-38 of Part One of this story. A more condensed but none the less interesting account of the presumed birth of the Great Lakes is to be found in Mill's "The International Geography," p. 741, under the section entitled "Niagara and the Great Lakes." Finally, a similar description, embellished by illuminating maps, can be found in the chapter on "The Pleistocene Period," p. 636 et seq., of Chamberlin and Salisbury's "Introductory Geology." The editions of the books here referred to will be found in the Bibliography, below.

An engaging account of the rôle of microbes in the segregation of iron deposits will be found in Professional Paper 113, of the United States Geological Survey, entitled "Iron-Depositing Bacteria and their Geologic Relations," by Edmund Cecil Harder. It is most unfortunate that there exists no trick of so turning back the clock of geologic time that Harder and other iron-microbiologists might be present during the actual laying-down of the immense hematite deposits of the Mis-sa-be Iron Range. Failing such a trick—and it must always, alas, remain impossible to experiment with the past—Harder's observations on today's activities of the iron microbes are certainly suggestive, as scientists like to say, if not entirely conclusive.

Appendix D: to Part Two

The map shown on pages 96-97, taken from the field minits of John E. and Cassius Merritt, will give the reader some idea of the thoroughness—no different from that of modern laboratory searchers—with which the Merritt boys conducted their dip-needle surveys. The data revealed by this map resulted, finally, in the discovery of the famous "Section 30" property on the Vermilion Iron Range. The ownership of this valuable mine was for decades in litigation, but now has been awarded to the Merritt heirs and the heirs of Eaton, Fagan, and others associated with Leonidas in his early explorations.

Appendix E: to Part Three

The flavor of John E. Merritt's poetry is best appreciated in conversation with him, or, rather, by listening to him as he recounts those old arduous days that preceded the discovery of the Mis-sa-be Iron Range. Extemporizing—and he has this in common with most non-professional tellers of folk tales—he is at his best. Yet, something of his strange combination of gentleness and vigor can perhaps be got from the following letter, written to this writer in the course of the investigations that preceded the composition of "Seven Iron Men."

"At Home,
November 1, 1928.

"Paul de Kruif,
New York.
"Dear Boy:

"Since I left you after the three-day camp we made . . . and there around our campfire met many of the old pathfinders of the Mis-sa-be and the then unknown north country, I have wondered if, in the hurried jumble of incidents I hurled at you, you were not entirely lost, and are now ever trying to untangle, straighten out, and connect up the abrupt places I ran you up against and left you there to find the way of the road out.

"Tonight I sit in the flickering light of our fire watching the battle of the shadows as they are driven back to the forest depths—and ever coming back, as our fire grows dim: I hear again the grind of that field of ice that forced us to take shelter on this inhospitable shore and how all through the night the grind of that floe as it was forced up over the rocks cutting to pieces the low cedar and alder growth that fringed the bank, the crash and roar of that breaking ice mingled with the ghostly complaint of the Norway pines kept us awake far into the night.

"To me all this brings haunting memories of those far off days, memories of men who laughed and sang and fought, of women who loved and dreamed and sorrowed. Men and women whom society has long since forgotten, whom God himself delighted to honor. Voyageurs in this, the unknown wilderness who were endowed with the best attributes God can give to a man—great physical strength, some imagination, and a love for a comrade as true and fine as is the love of a man for his mate. Most of these old pathfinders—these old voyageurs—have long since paid a debt which all must pay, and it is my pleasure to believe that the final reckoning was entirely satisfactory and the Great Creditor allotted to them a high place in his esteem, and it was a sufficient reward to the debtor when he heard 'Well done, old voyageur. Pitch your camp by yon mystic lake and rest you here forever.'

"I made an effort, in the little time we had, to give you a glimpse of some of the unwritten history in this great drama whose chief actors were jus simple woodsmen, men who fought and subdued a great labyrinth of tangled, unbroken forest, a forest that had long stood guard over the great wealth that lay hidden 'neath its shade and whose deep roots were anchored with bands of iron. Yes, these men toiled, planned, and made beasts of burden of themselves, that this hidden treasure might be brought forth and replace this wilderness with an empire that now maintains thousands of happy homes in their clustering cities and villages.

" . . . I want first of all to have you meet and become acquainted with all those men who fought to conquer this wilderness, and who in the end lost all, and yet came through the ordeal as only such rugged characters could come. Shorn, it is true, of a hard-earned fortune, but rich beyond computation in the love and esteem of their friends and neighbors. Surely a treasury filled to bursting with this commodity.

"I want you to meet them on the trail—voyage with them up unknown rivers—help them cut portages—and carry over to the next stream that will bear them through the unknown and camp on the shores of a lake where none but the red man had ever pushed the prow of his canoe.

"It seems to me as I sit here tonight, that the task you have undertaken is so tremendous, the trail you are to traverse so intricate in places, so dim that in order to find your way out you should know personally the class of men who discovered this hidden treasure, and finally forced a skeptical world to acknowledge a condition new in mineralogy, new in methods and practice, and all founded on a theory based wholly on observation and crude reasoning.

"Doctor Paul, I had no time to tell you this story. It would take me much longer than the parts of three days we enjoyed together. It must come to you in patches, put together as our mothers made the old patchwork quilts, that kept you and me snug and warm. . . . So from now on you and I are going to camp together—canoe up unknown streams, run rapids that in our sane moments we would avoid, build rafts and wreck in midstream, get lost, freeze in the snows of winter, melt in the scorching heat

224

of summer, starve, carry our pardner miles through a featherbed or muskeg swamp, watch with him when near death, on a sand barren with a wind howling 50 miles and coming straight from the ice fields of the Arctic.

"You dear old voyageur I will make you so darned tired and weary on this one voyage I fear you will never consent to take another one with me. When you have had enough, just say so, then in after years there will come to Paul and John very pleasant memories of all the campfires along the trail and of all the many and wonderful changes that we will both note can happen in the short life of the ordinary man. Throw on another hunk of wood, boy, and let's turn in.

"Good night.
"John E."

Appendix F: to Part Four

An adequate summary of the Reverend Mr. Gates's philanthropic achievements is presented in an editorial in the New York *World*, for Friday, February 8, 1929:

"The whole world knows what the fortune of John D. Rockefeller has accomplished since he made his first great gift in 1889—$600,000 for the projected University of Chicago. Comparatively few know how much the imagination and foresight of Frederick T. Gates, who has just died, did to fructify the Rockefeller millions. He conceived, planned, and gave business organization to some of the greatest of Mr. Rockefeller's benefactions. He was for twenty-seven years before his retirement in 1917 one of the world's leaders in large scale philanthropy.

"A tremendous fortune can be wisely spent only by the aid of men of trained vision, tireless industry and a strong sense of the practical. The young Baptist clergyman and denominational executive from the Middle West who so impressed Mr. Rockefeller by his handling of University of

Chicago affairs had just the needed combination of qualities. He, Goodspeed and Mr. Rockefeller may be called the founders of the University of Chicago. He, inspired by an article of Dr. Osler's, worked out for Mr. Rockefeller the plan for the Rockefeller Institute. It was he, again, with William H. Baldwin and several others, who organized the General Education Board and obtained Mr. Rockefeller's support; he was its chairman for a decade. He was one of the architects of the Rockefeller Foundation, which has created so many subsidiary philanthropies. When he retired it was estimated that he had already been responsible for the spending of some 175 millions.

"Small sums of money can be distributed in familiar ways. But those who amass our greatest modern fortunes must discover new fields and devise new machinery. They are fortunate if they have the aid of men like Mr. Gates."

This splendid tribute develops, in words which failed the present writer, a portrait or sketch of the Reverend Mr. Gates as a discoverer, so to speak.

Appendix G: to Part Four

Those wishing to pursue further the peculiar controversy as to whether Mr. Rockefeller talked to Leonidas only about the weather and purely social matters, as the Reverend Mr. Gates insisted, or whether Mr. Rockefeller laid before Leonidas a plan of consolidation of his own properties with those of the Merritt brothers, as Lon maintained, may consult the following sources:

The Reverend Mr. Gates has stated his side of the matter in his testimony in the trial of the suit at law of Alfred Merritt vs. John D. Rockefeller, the trial of which was had, beginning on the fifth day of June, A.D. 1895, in the Circuit Court of the United States, District of Minnesota, 5th Division. The bound court records of this celebrated case are exceedingly scarce, but their perusal will certainly repay the interested investigator for his pains to get at them.

The Reverend Mr. Gates has further elaborated his version of the unquestioned meeting between Leonidas and Mr. John D. Rockefeller in a long statement entitled "Inside Story of Rockefeller and Mis-sa-be Mines." This appeared in the Magazine Section of the Philadelphia *Public Ledger*, Sunday morning, January 21, 1912.

Lon's version of the famous meeting is to be found in his testimony in the lawsuit above-mentioned, and it will further be found, set forth in full, in his testimony before the Committee on Investigation of the United States Steel Corporation, Vol. III, pp. 1899 and 1900. See "Sources of Information" below.

Both Leonidas and the Reverend Mr. Gates have now passed on, and from them nothing more can be heard, in our quest to prove who was right and who mistaken. Nevertheless, it may interest those who have not been daunted in their search through the above sources, to turn to pp. 601-4 of the transcript of Record 707, in the case of John D. Rockefeller, Plaintiff in Error, versus Alfred Merritt, Defendant in Error. This is the copy of a letter, dated Duluth, Minnesota, Nov. 3, 1893, and written by Leonidas Merritt to F. T. Gates. It is true that the curious may find this long journey through legal documents trying, and at times dull. Yet the pursuit of truth through these mazes of contradiction and error may not be without reward.

Appendix H: to Part Four

Lon's best known poem is unquestionably that entitled "Ne-Con-Dis," but on account of its controversial tone, and its great length, the present writer feels it best not to include it in these mild, and as nearly as possible impartial notes, in spite of its undoubted vigor, its picturesque use of Indian words, and its appalling sarcasm and vituperative power. It is more seemly, perhaps, to leave the reader with an idea of Lon in a more gently reminiscent mood: consequently this little history of one of Leonidas's last hunts—of course a fruitless one—for iron, is here appended.

THE VOYAGEUR

Listen to me, whoever may care,
While I sing the song of the voyageur.

In the gloam of even one wintry day,
They crossed the mouth of Old South Bay;
Salt and Pepper and John and Lon,
Off the rock-bound coast of old Nipigon.

Off the beetling crags in their light canoe,
The sea rolled high and the north wind blew;
Joe Salt low down in the stern sheets set,
Joe Pepper forward, with spray all wet.

Now in the trough, its great green wall
Threat'ning to break and o'erwhelm us all;
Now on the crest of the breaking sea,
Salt and Pepper and you and me.

In silence they bent to the springing oar,
Midst the blinding spray and the tempest roar,
And felt the wild thrill of the water's rave
That bore us aloft on the foam-crested wave.

We worked, Johnny Boy, on our knees in the waist,
Till we felt in our mouths the coppery taste;
We worked, Johnny Boy, for the opposite shore,
Till our sinews and nerves were knotted and sore.

And at last down the slope of a high-rolling sea,
We slid to the calm of a saving lea;

SEVEN IRON MEN

With one wild yell, which echoed back
To the roaring wind and the tempest wrack.

A moment a-tremble our good boat lay,
Then shook her wet sides, as if to say:
"Gallant Boat, Gallant Crew, from stern to bow,
Blow on you Beggar, blow winds, blow."

Brightly that night did our campfire shine
On the whirling snow and the wind-rocked pine:
Under the pall of a scowling sky
We lay in our blankets warm and dry.

Safe in the camp on the shores of old Nipigon
Salt and Pepper and John and Lon
Smoked to the roll of the restless deep.
Then sank to the rest of a dreamless sleep.

Such is the luck of the Voyageur,
Sung for the ear of Who-may-care.

LON MERRITT for JOHN MERRITT.

It was on this cruise that John E. Merritt remembers
Lon yelling, during the very worst of the storm, at the
same time pointing to the Indian Joe Salt in the stern:
"Is he whistlin', Johnnie, is he still whistlin'?" John yelled
back that Joe was still whistling. "All right," answered
Lon. "All right, Johnnie, so long as he's whistlin'. But
when he begins to say 'ts-ts-ts-ts' I'm biddin' you good-
by!"

SOURCES OF INFORMATION

Audubon, J. J. "Delineations of American Scenery and Character." Baker, 1926.

Bridge, J. H. "The Inside History of the Carnegie Steel Company." Aldine, 1903.

Brunhes, J. "Human Geography." Rand McNally, 1920.

Carnegie, A. Testimony before the Stanley Committee on Investigation of United States Steel Corporation, United States House of Representatives, in 8 Volumes; Vol. III, pp. 2345-2467. Gov't Printing Office, 1912.

Chamberlin, T. C., and Salisbury, R. D. "College Textbook of Geology." Part I: Geological Processes and their Results, rewritten and revised by R. T. Chamberlin and Paul MacClintock. Holt, 1927.

—— "Introductory Geology." Holt, 1924.

Chester, A. H. "The Romance of the Ranges." Article, 1914, reprinted in Van Brunt's "Duluth and St. Louis County." (*See* Van Brunt.)

Clark, N. M. "He Knew Millions Were There Before He Saw a Bit of Ore." Interview with Leonidas Merritt, *American Magazine*, 1923.

Clements, J. M. "The Vermilion Iron-Bearing District of Minnesota." Monograph XLV, The U. S. Geological Survey, 1903. Gov't Printing Office, 1903.

Cotton, J. Testimony before the Stanley Committee on

Investigation of the United States Steel Corporation, United States House of Representatives . . . Vol. III, pp. 2225-2300. Gov't Printing Office, 1911.

Culkin, W. E. Biographical Material on George Stuntz, in Collection of St. Louis County Historical Society. N. d.

Davis, W. M. "Physical Geography." Ginn, 1898.

—— "The United States." Chapter in Mill's "The International Geography." Appleton, 1919.

De la Blache, P. V. "Principles of Human Geography." Holt, 1926.

Ellis, C. E., "Iron Ranges of Minnesota." Historical Souvenir of the Virginia Enterprise. 1909.

Gates, F. T., The Reverend. "Inside Story of Rockefeller and Mis-sa-be Mines." Philadelphia *Public Ledger*, Sunday, Jan. 21, 1912, Magazine Section.

(Note: This story appeared at this time in numerous papers throughout the United States, and may be taken to be Messrs. Gates and Rockefeller's formal answer to Alfred and Lon's testimony before the Stanley Committee, after Mr. Rockefeller and the Reverend Mr. Gates had declined to testify before that body. This story was later embodied in a pamphlet entitled "The Truth about Mr. Rockefeller and the Merritts," widely distributed.)

—— Letter to Congressman A. O. Stanley, declining to testify before the Stanley Committee, 1911. Newspaper clipping in Scrapbook in Merritt Family Archives.

—— Testimony in Court Record of Suit at Law of Alfred Merritt vs. John D. Rockefeller, June, 1895, Circuit Court of U. S., District of Minnesota, 5th Div.

Geikie, Sir A. "The Founders of Geology." Macmillan, 1905.

Harder, E. C. "Iron-Depositing Bacteria and their Geological Relations." Professional Paper 113, The U. S. Geological Survey. Gov't Printing Office, 1919.

Harvey, G. "Henry Clay Frick *The Man.*" Scribner, 1928.

Henry, A. "Travels and Adventures in Canada and the Indian Territories between the Years 1760 and 1776, in Two Parts." Riley, 1809.

Hobbs, W. H. "The Late Glacial and Post-Glacial Uplift of the Michigan Basin." Publication 5, Geological Series 3, Michigan Geological and Biological Survey. 1911.

Hulbert, A. B. "The Paths of Inland Commerce." Yale University Press, 1920.

Leith, C. K. "The Mesabi Iron-Bearing District." Monograph XLIII, The U. S. Geological Survey. Gov't Printing Office, 1903.

—— *See also* Van Hise and Leith.

Leverett, F., and Taylor, F. B. "The Pleistocene of Indiana and Michigan and the History of the Great Lakes." Monograph LIII, The U. S. Geological Survey. Gov't Printing Office, 1915.

Martin, L. "The Pleistocene." Chapter XVI in Monograph LII, The U. S. Geological Survey. Gov't Printing Office, 1911.

Martz, C. H. Testimony before the Stanley Committee on Investigation of the United States Steel Corporation, United States House of Representatives . . . Vol. III, pp. 1819-1845. Gov't Printing Office, 1911.

Merritt, A. Autobiographical Notes. Typescript, Collection of St. Louis County Historical Society, 1917.

—— Testimony in Court Record of Suit at Law of Alfred Merritt vs. John D. Rockefeller, June, 1895, Circuit Court of U. S., Dist. of Minnesota, 5th Div.

—— Testimony before the Stanley Committee on Investigation of the United States Steel Corporation,

SEVEN IRON MEN

United States House of Representatives . . . Vol.
III, pp. 1845-1884. Gov't Printing Office, 1911.

Merritts, Family of. Biographical Sketches, *Duluth Daily
Commonwealth*, entitled "Seven Sons of One House."
May 24, 1893.

Merritt, J. E. Letters, Typescript, unpublished, to A. R.
Merritt, 1912. Merritt Family Archives.

—— Memoirs, Typescript, unpublished, 1928-9. Merritt
Family Archives.

—— "The Voyageur's Dream." A Poem, Typescript, unpublished. Merritt Family Archives.

Merritt, L. "Memoranda of an Interview with J. D. Rockefeller at his office about the middle of June, 1893."
Typescript, unpublished, Merritt Family Archives.

—— "Ne-con-dis." Mimeographed, unpublished, dated
Oct. 1, 1895, Merritt Family Archives.

—— New Sectional Map of the Mineral District of Minnesota, 1890. Merritt Family Archives. Published by
Lon Merritt.

—— "Outline History of my Connections with Biwabik
Mountain Iron Company." Typescript, unpublished,
dated Oct. 25, 1894. Merritt Family Archives.

—— "Outline History of the Discovery and Development
of the Mis-sa-be Iron Range and the Merritts' Con-
nection with the Same." Typescript; unpublished;
dated June 7, 1894. Merritt Family Archives.

—— Scrapbooks. Merrit Family Archives.
(Note: These are five in number, very bulky and
nearly completely filled, containing most valuable historical material in form of letters, mementoes, and
otherwise unobtainable newspaper clippings of date
from middle '80's onward. They are peculiar for their
completeness, their impartiality, in that Lon inserted
all material no matter how derogatory to himself and
the Merritts, as well as accounts of their triumphs,
and other eulogistic material.)

—— Testimony before the Stanley Committee on Investigation of the United States Steel Corporation, U. S. House of Representatives . . . Vol. III, pp. 1885-1934. Gov't Printing Office, 1911.

—— Testimony in Court Record of Suit at Law of Alfred Merritt vs. John D. Rockefeller. June, 1895, Circuit Court of U. S., District of Minnesota, 5th Div.

—— "To Whomsoever It May Concern." (A Reply to the Reverend Mr. F. T. Gates's Pamphlet entitled "The Truth about Mr. Rockefeller and the Merritts.") Typescript, unpublished, dated March, 1912. Merritt Family Archives.

Mill, H. R. The International Geography. Appleton, 1919.

Myers, G. "The History of the Great American Fortunes." In 3 vols. Kerr, 1907-09.

Osborn, C. S. Address at the Joint Meeting of the Lake Superior Mining Institute and the Iron and Steel Division of the American Institute of Mining and Metallurgical Engineers, at Iron Mountain, Michigan, Sept. 8, 1928.

—— "The Earth Upsets." Waverly Press, 1927.

—— "The Iron Hunter." Macmillan, 1919.

Phillips, S. A. "Sidelights on James J. Hill." Quoted in *The Evening Telegram*, July 13, 1901, from *Minneapolis Journal*, May 25, 1894.

Pumpelly, R. "My Reminiscences." Holt, 1918.

Rockefeller, J. D. Deposition, in Court Record of Suit at Law of Alfred Merritt vs. John D. Rockefeller, June, 1895, Circuit Court of U. S., District of Minnesota, 5th Div.

—— Letter to Congressman A. O. Stanley, declining to testify before the Stanley Committee, 1911. Newspaper Clipping in Scrapbook in Merritt Family Archives.

Rockefeller, J. D. "Random Reminiscences of Men and Events." Doubleday, Page, 1909.
Sandburg, C. "The American Songbag." Harcourt, Brace, 1927.
Sargent, W. C. Personal Communication, *re* G. R. Stuntz, Dec. 26, 1928.
Shaler, N. S. "Man and the Earth." Duffield, 1917.
—— (with collaborators). "The United States of America: A Study of the American Commonwealth, Its National Resources, People, Industries, Manufactures, Commerce, and Its Work in Literature, Science, Education and Self-Government." Appleton, 1894.
Smith, J. R. "North America." Harcourt, Brace, 1925.
Stanley, A. O. Hearings before the Committee on Investigation of the United States Steel Corporation, U. S. House of Representatives . . . Vol. III, pp. 1603-2468. Gov't Printing Office, 1911-12.
Stuntz, G. R. "Mound Builders." Read before Minnesota Academy of Natural Sciences, Jan. 6, 1895. Collection of St. Louis Historical Society.
—— "On Evidences of Early Man in Northeast Minnesota." Read before Minnesota Academy of Natural Sciences, Dec. 2, 1884. Collection of St. Louis Historical Society.
—— "On Some Recent Geological Changes in Northeastern Wisconsin." Proc. Amer. Assoc. Adv. of Sc., Vol. LXXVIII, 1870, pp. 206-7. Quoted by Hobbs.
Turner, F. J. "The Frontier in American History." Holt, 1920.
Van Brunt, W. "Duluth and St. Louis County, Minnesota." The American Historical Society, 1921.
Van Hise, C. R., and Leith, C. K. "The Geology of the Lake Superior Region. Monograph LII, The U. S. Geological Survey. Gov't Printing Office, 1911.

SEVEN IRON MEN

Walker, J. B. "The Story of Steel." Harper, 1926.

Winchell, H. V. "Report on the Mesabi Iron Range in Minnesota." Extract from Twentieth Annual Report, Minnesota Geological Survey, reprinted and re-paged. IV: 1892.

NOTE: In addition to the above list of principal sources, it is well to mention innumerable interviews with miners, explorers, capitalists, and Great Lakes sailors—who must, excepting my friend, Mr. Roy O. Fritsche, remain anonymous, but whose contributions were most valuable. Also, hundreds of separate and isolated newspaper accounts of the stirring days of the discovery of the Vermilion and Mis-sa-be Ranges were studied in the admirable files of the Collection of the St. Louis County Historical Society. These are far too numerous to list separately.

INDEX

237

INDEX

Fay, George, 99
Florada, E., 171
Forbes, The Rev. Dr., 167
Frick, H. C., has interview with Leonidas, 145-148; buys large part of Oliver Mining Company against Carnegie's wishes, 177-181; other references to, 155, 192, 204
Fritsche, R. O., 236

Gates, The Rev. Fred T., architect of Rockefeller Foundation, 226; a great organizer of philanthropy, 190-191; allays Merritt's suspicions, 197; becomes enthusiastic about Merritt iron properties, 190-191; comes to rescue of Merritts, 195; declines to defend name before Stanley Committee, 209; defends Mr. Rockefeller against charges of fraud, 209; eulogized as eleemosynar, 191; eulogy of, by New York *World*, 225-226; kindly helps Leonidas to raise money on mines, 194-195; lauds good faith of Mr. Rockefeller, 205; logic of, 210; organizes General Education Board, 226; responsible for spending one hundred and seventy-five millions of Mr. Rockefeller's money, 226; works out plan of Rockefeller Institute, 226
Gailey, Mr., 181
Gallionella, 77, 78, 214, 215
Gardner, Congressman, 201
Geggie, the cruiser, 82
Gill, Captain, wounds his wife, 153, 167
God, 77, 193, 224
Goff, Gil, 82
Gogebic Iron Range, 117, 121
Goodspeed, Dr., 226
Grant, Donald, 152, 162, 183, 184, 187
Guthrie and Foley, Messrs., 152, 162

Hale, J. T., 152
Hall, Edwin, 6

Harder, E. C., 221
Harrison, M. B., 93
Harvey, Col. George, 180, 200, 204
Hibbing, Frank, 152
Hill, James J., 31, 157, 215
Hobbs, W. H., 217-218
Holley, Mr., 192
Housell, Mr., the cook, 129; cashes in, 202
Houston, Sam, 203
Humphreys, A. E., 152

Iron, deposited by microbes, 67
Irving, geologist, 81
Isabella, the blast furnace, 53

Jones, Capt. Bill, 52, 192
Jones, Johnny, 151, 154

Kimberly, Peter, 154-155; leases Biwabik from Merritts, 170; other references to, 184
Kitchi Gammi, 3, 42, 149, 200, 210, 213

Leith, C. K., 220
Leverett, Frank, 221
Loeb, Jacques, 220
Longfellow, H. W., 149
Loon Foot, Chief, 8-10
Lucy, the blast furnace, 53

McCaskill, John, 130-132, 135
McDougall, Capt. Alex., 186
McKinley, John, 131-133, 134, 135, 141
Mallman, the cruiser, 82
Marquette Iron Range, 121
Martz, Charles, 162
Menominee Iron Range, 121
Merritts, family of, as laughing-stock of Duluth, 121, 122; begin steamshovel mining, 141; build fifteen hundred ore cars for D. M. and N., 185; enter consolidation with Mr. Rockefeller, 196; real monuments to, 213, 214; receive five hundred thousand dollars from Mr. Rockefeller after retraction, 209; sign retraction of charges

238

INDEX

241

PAUL DE KRUIF (1890–1971) was a bacteriologist at the University of Michigan and the best-selling author of more than a dozen books, including *Microbe Hunters, Hunger Fighters,* and *Men against Death.* His articles on science and medicine were published in magazines such as *Country Gentleman, Ladies' Home Journal,* and *Reader's Digest.*